THE REVELS PLAYS

THE CARDINAL

JAMES SHIRLEY

Edited by

E. M. Yearling

MANCHESTER
UNIVERSITY PRESS

© the estate of E. M. Yearling 1986
All rights reserved
Published by Manchester University Press
Oxford Road, Manchester M13 9PL, UK

British Library Cataloguing in Publication Data
Shirley, James
  The Cardinal.—(The Revels plays)
  I. Title   II. Yearling, E.M.   III. Series
  822'.4   PR3144.C3
        ISBN 0-7190-1537-5 *cased*

Typeset by August Filmsetting, Haydock, St. Helens
Printed in Great Britain
by Bell and Bain Ltd., Glasgow

Contents

FRONTISPIECE   Fol. 15r of *Don Manuell*, an early version of *The Court Secret*. The insertion in the left-hand margin is probably in Shirley's own handwriting. Reproduced by permission of the Provost and Fellows of Worcester College, Oxford.

General Editors' Preface

The series known as the Revels Plays was conceived by Clifford Leech. The idea for the series emerged in his mind, as he explained in his preface to the first of the Revels Plays in 1958, from the success of the New Arden Shakespeare. The aim of the new group of texts was 'to apply to Shakespeare's predecessors, contemporaries and successors the methods that are now used in Shakespeare editing'. The plays chosen were to include well known works from the early Tudor period to about 1700, as well as others less familiar but of literary and theatrical merit: 'the plays included,' Leech wrote, 'should be such as to deserve and indeed demand performance.' We owe it to Clifford Leech that the idea became reality. He set the high standards of the series, ensuring that editors of individual volumes produced work of lasting merit, equally useful for teachers and students, theatre directors and actors. Clifford Leech remained General Editor until 1971, and was succeeded by F. David Hoeniger, who retired in 1985.

The Revels Plays are now under the direction of four General Editors, E. A. J. Honigmann, J. R. Mulryne, David Bevington and E. M. Waith. The publishers, originally Methuen, are now Manchester University Press. Despite these changes, the format and essential character of the series will continue, and it is hoped that its editorial standards will be maintained. Except for some work in progress, the General Editors intend, in expanding the series, to concentrate for the immediate future on plays from the period 1558–1642, and may include a small number of non-dramatic works of interest to students of drama. Some slight changes have been forced by considerations of cost. For example, in editions from 1978, notes to the introduction are placed together at the end, not at the foot of the page. Collation and commentary notes will continue, however, to appear on the relevant pages.

The text of each Revels play, in accordance with established practice in the series, is edited afresh from the original text of best authority (in a few instances, texts), but spelling and punctuation are modernised and speech headings are silently made consistent. Elisions in the original are also silently regularised, except where metre would be affected by the change; since 1968 the '-ed' form is used for non-syllabic terminations in past tenses and past participles ('-'d' earlier), and '-èd' for syllabic ('-ed' earlier). The editor emends, as distinct from modernises, his original only in instances where error is patent, or at least very probable, and correction persuasive. Act divisions are given only if they appear in the original or if the structure of the play clearly points to them. Those act and scene divisions not found in the original are provided unobtrusively in small type and in square brackets. Square brackets are also used for any other additions to or changes in the stage directions of the original.

Revels Plays do not provide a variorum collation, but only those variants which require the critical attention of serious textual students. All departures of substance from 'copy-text' are listed, including any relineation and those changes in punctuation which involve to any degree a decision between alternative interpretations; but not such accidentals as turned letters, nor necessarily additions to stage directions whose editorial nature is already made clear by the use of brackets. Press corrections in the 'copy-text' are likewise included. Of later emendations of the text, only those are given which as alternative readings still deserve attention.

One of the hallmarks of the Revels Plays is the thoroughness of their annotations. Besides explaining the meaning of difficult words and passages, the editor provides comments on customs or usage, text or stage-business—indeed, on anything he judges pertinent and helpful. Each volume contains a Glossarial Index to the Commentary, in which particular attention is drawn to meanings for words not listed in *O.E.D.*

The Introduction to a Revels play assesses the authority of the 'copy-text' on which it is based, and discusses the editorial methods employed in dealing with it; the editor also considers his play's date and (where relevant) sources, together with its place in the work of the author and in the theatre of its time. Stage history is offered, and in the case of a play by an author not previously represented in the series a brief biography is given.

It is our hope that plays edited in this fashion will promote further scholarly and theatrical investigation of one of the richest periods in theatrical history.

E. A. J. HONIGMANN
J. R. MULRYNE
DAVID BEVINGTON
E. M. WAITH

Preface

I owe a long-standing debt to the late Professor James Arnott, who first interested me in Shirley, and to Professor Ian Donaldson, who guided that early interest. From my General Editor, Professor Ernst Honigmann, came the opportunity to renew my acquaintance with Shirley. I am grateful for his encouragement and his patient answers to even the most trivial of queries. My thanks are also due to the many librarians who sent me microfilms or extended their facilities for study. I am particularly grateful to the staff of Special Collections at Glasgow University; to Bruce Whiteman of McMaster University; to Lesley Montgomery of Worcester College, Oxford; to C. D. W. Sheppard of the Brotherton Library, University of Leeds; to Dorothy Swerdlove, Curator of the Theatre Collection in the New York Public Library; to the librarians at the William Andrews Clark Memorial Library, University of California, and at the Turnbull Library, Wellington, New Zealand, who collated copies of *The Cardinal* for me; and to the Wing Revision Project. The Magic Theatre of San Francisco furnished me generously with publicity material and newspaper cuttings.

I have been helped by many friends and colleagues; by Maev Alexander, Sandra Billington, Robert Casto, Robert Cummings, Donald Mackenzie, Alison and Stephen Rawles, Mary and Rick Shaner, Hilary Smith, and my husband, Alec Yearling. Ronald Huebert, who is editing *The Lady of Pleasure* for the Revels Series, has kindly shared with me some of his material and a great deal of enthusiasm.

A grant from the British Academy made it possible for me to visit a group of American libraries, and from Glasgow University has come a generous combination of study leave and grants for travel and for microfilms.

For permission to publish a photograph from the manuscript, *Don Manuell*, I thank the Provost and Fellows of Worcester College, Oxford. I am also grateful for permission to publish details of a Restoration cast list from the copy of *The Cardinal* in The Brotherton Collection, University of Leeds.

E. M. YEARLING, University of Glasgow.

My wife did not live to see her edition through the press, and I am most grateful to Professor Ernst Honigmann and to the editorial staff at Manchester University Press for their advice and assistance.

A. E. YEARLING

Abbreviations

SHIRLEY: EDITIONS COLLATED

Oct.	*The Cardinal* (1652) in *Six New Playes* (London, 1653).
Corr.	Corrected forme.
Uncorr.	Uncorrected forme.
Gifford	*The Dramatic Works and Poems of James Shirley*, ed. William Gifford and Alexander Dyce, 6 vols. (London, 1833).
Gosse	*James Shirley*, ed. Edmund Gosse, Mermaid Series (London, 1888).
Neilson	*The Chief Elizabethan Dramatists excluding Shakespeare*, ed. William A. Neilson (Boston, 1911).
Walley	*Early Seventeenth-Century Plays, 1600–1642*, ed. Harold R. Walley and John H. Wilson (New York, 1930).
Brooke	*English Drama, 1580–1642*, ed. C. F. Tucker Brooke and Nathaniel B. Paradise (New York, 1933).
Baskervill	*Elizabethan and Stuart Plays*, ed. Charles R. Baskervill, Virgil B. Heltzel, and Arthur H. Nethercot (New York, 1934).
Parks	*The English Drama, 900–1642*, ed. E. Winfield Parks and Richmond C. Beatty (New York, 1935).
Forker	*The Cardinal*, ed. Charles R. Forker (Bloomington, Ind., 1964).
Lawrence	*Jacobean and Caroline Tragedies*, ed. Robert G. Lawrence (London, 1975).

OTHER

Abbott	E. A. Abbott, *A Shakespearian Grammar* (1869), 3rd. ed. (London, repr. 1888).
Armstrong	*The Poems of James Shirley*, ed. Ray L. Armstrong (New York, 1941).
Bas	Georges Bas, *James Shirley (1596–1666): Dramaturge Caroléen* (Lille, 1973).
Beaumont and Fletcher, *Wks*.	*The Works of Francis Beaumont and John Fletcher*, ed. A. Glover and A. R. Waller, 10 vols. (Cambridge, 1905–12).
Bentley	Gerald E. Bentley, *The Jacobean and Caroline Stage*, 7 vols. (Oxford, 1941–68).
Bentley, *Profession*	Gerald E. Bentley, *The Profession of Dramatist in Shakespeare's Time, 1590–1642* (Princeton, 1971).
Boas	F. S. Boas, *An Introduction to Stuart Drama* (London, 1946).

Bowers   Fredson Bowers, *Elizabethan Revenge Tragedy, 1587–1642* (Princeton, 1940).

C.S.P.D.   *Calendar of State Papers*, Domestic Series.

Dekker, *Wks.*   Thomas Dekker, *Dramatic Works*, ed. Fredson Bowers, 4 vols. (Cambridge, 1953–61).

E.S.   *English Studies.*

Forsythe   Robert S. Forsythe, *The Relations of Shirley's Plays to the Elizabethan Drama* (New York, 1914).

Herbert   *The Dramatic Records of Sir Henry Herbert*, ed. Joseph Q. Adams (New Haven, 1917).

H.L.Q.   *Huntington Library Quarterly.*

J.E.G.P.   *Journal of English and Germanic Philology.*

Jonson, *Wks.*   *Ben Jonson*, ed. C. H. Herford and Percy and Evelyn Simpson, 11 vols. (Oxford, 1925–52).

Massinger,   *The Plays and Poems of Philip Massinger*, ed. Philip
   Plays   Edwards and Colin Gibson, 5 vols. (Oxford, 1976).

M.P.   *Modern Philology*

Nason   Arthur H. Nason, *James Shirley, Dramatist* (New York, 1915).

N.& Q.   *Notes and Queries.*

O.E.D.   *Oxford English Dictionary.*

P.M.L.A.   *Publications of the Modern Language Association of America.*

R.E.S.   *Review of English Studies.*

S.B.   *Studies in Bibliography.*

S.E.L.   *Studies in English Literature, 1500–1900.*

Sh.S.   *Shakespeare Survey.*

Stone   Lawrence Stone, *The Crisis of the Aristocracy, 1558–1641* (Oxford, 1965).

Tilley   Morris P. Tilley, *A Dictionary of the Proverbs in England in the Sixteenth and Seventeenth Centuries* (Ann Arbor, 1950).

T.N.   *Theatre Notebook.*

Wing   *Short-Title Catalogue of Books Printed in England, Scotland, Ireland, Wales . . . 1641–1700*, compiled by Donald Wing, 3 vols. (New York, 1945–51), and 2nd ed., revised and enlarged, vol. 1 (1972).

Wood   Anthony Wood, *Athenae Oxonienses*, 2nd ed., 2 vols. (London, 1721).

Shakespeare is quoted from the Tudor Shakespeare, ed. Peter Alexander (London, 1951). All drastically abridged play-titles are Shakespearian and can be found in Onions, *A Shakespeare Glossary* (London, repr. 1966). Other well-known play-titles have minor cuts. References to other Shirley plays are to Gifford and consist of act and scene numbers followed by volume and page numbers. References to the following plays are to Revels editions: *Bussy D'Ambois, The Changeling, The Duchess of Malfi, The Fawn, The Malcontent, The Revenger's Tragedy, Tamburlaine, 'Tis Pity She's a Whore, The White Devil, The Widow's Tears, A Woman Killed with Kindness.*

Introduction

James Shirley was born in London in 1596 and died there in 1666. We know a good deal about his life. He failed to distinguish himself at Merchant Taylors' School and spent two years as the servant of a scrivener, Thomas Frith, before attending Cambridge. After graduating he was ordained, but in 1621 he became a schoolmaster in St Albans, an occupation which underpinned his first years as a dramatist and helped to restore his fortune when the Puritans later destroyed his theatrical livelihood and his king.[1] He moved to London in the mid 1620's, to a successful but perhaps disappointing dramatic career. Early hopes of the highest reward culminated in the presentation at Whitehall by the Inns of Court of *The Triumph of Peace* (1633/4) but were almost simultaneously stifled by the reappearance in London and in the court's especial favour of Davenant, who in 1638 gained the Poet Laureateship that might otherwise have gone to Shirley.[2] In the autumn of 1636, Shirley found himself jobless when his company, the Queen's Men, disbanded, and he travelled to Dublin to help found the Werburgh Street Theatre.[3] Then in 1640 Massinger died, and Shirley replaced him as chief dramatist of the King's Men at Blackfriars; but he returned to prominence only to witness the stage's rapid decline. Two years later, Puritan fiat closed the theatres. Shirley's support for the Royalists brought impeachment and a fine of £1, allegedly a sixth of his capital, but his later teaching and publishing ventures—several plays and a Latin grammar—left a considerable sum to be distributed in his will.[4] Death came dramatically for Shirley and his second wife, 'overcome with Affrightments, Disconsolations, and other Miseries',[5] after escaping the Fire of London.

Shirley's large and regular output ranges from competent potboilers to a near masterpiece in *The Lady of Pleasure*.[6] Least stimulating are his tragicomedies. Through these trudge a succession of unrecognised lost heirs, loyal and suffering ladies, imprisoned lovers, harsh monarchs and unscrupulous favourites; their adventures are sub-Fletcherian and their occasional threatened incests have much to do with plot and nothing to do with psychology. Yet, as Georges Bas

I

points out (p. 168), between 1632 and 1636 the tragicomedies were paired with lively and original comedies. *Hyde Park*, *The Ball*, *The Gamester*, *The Example* and *The Lady of Pleasure* all present the places, pastimes and people of Caroline London. Their dialogue and action are witty, and they vividly depict the would-be fast set at play—betting on races in *Hyde Park*, gambling compulsively in *The Gamester*, attending fashionable evening parties in *The Ball*. Tragedy seems less to have attracted Shirley.[7] Three tragedies were written by 1631. *The Politician* and *The Cardinal* follow almost a decade later.[8] There is in the tragedies the merest hint of experimentation, of trying not to do the same thing twice (Bas, p. 140). Two are love tragedies, but whereas *The Maid's Revenge* is a tale of violent desires and jealousies, complicated by an Iberian sense of honour and culminating in madness and multiple deaths, *Love's Cruelty* portrays a quieter domestic disaster of adultery and delayed murder. *The Traitor* and *The Politician* are both stories of political intrigue laced with sex; in both, a wicked favourite attempts to gain power. In *The Traitor* a trio of tainted characters are destroyed in the last scene's bloodbath, but *The Politician* is a calmer affair in which the deaths of the villains, Gotharus and Queen Marpisa, leave the weak king, his son Turgesius, and Gotharus' virtuous wife, Albina, in control of a kingdom disturbed but not devastated. *The Cardinal*, Shirley's last tragedy, combines love and politics in a straightforward revenge plot. It could be, and has been seen as the last of a long line of Jacobean revenge plays. Yet by his presentation of a recognisable ordinary world Shirley achieves something different from most of his predecessors' tragedies.

There is nothing extraordinary about Shirley's success story; achievement, but never quite the highest;[9] plays written with talent and craftsmanship rather than with genius; financial security established, lost, and won again. His life spanned years of change and upheaval but since his work as a playwright was confined to Charles I's reign he is tidily excluded from the dark fascinations of Jacobean drama and the witty irreverence of the Restoration. After 1642 his only play was *Honoria and Mammon*, an expanded version of the earlier masque, *The Contention for Honour and Riches* (*c.* 1631), and so we have little indication of whether hardship would have affected the balanced clarity of his writing. Yet when he wrote *The Cardinal* the stage which was his living and the stable world he knew were already threatened.[10]

II. DATE AND INFLUENCES

The King's Men performed a Shirley play at each end of the Black-friars season from June 1640 till the theatres were closed in September 1642. *The Cardinal* was licensed on 25 November 1641,[11] and was that season's winter play. Many sources and influences have been suggested; few have been agreed on. They include Lope de Vega's *El buen vecino* and Samuel Harding's *Sicily and Naples*; Jacobean revenge drama in general and *The Duchess of Malfi* in particular; and Archbishop Laud's part in contemporary events.

El buen vecino has been proposed as the source of the main plot.[12] César, heir to the throne of Naples, loves Elena but fears that the king will marry her to a previous admirer, Carlos, Count of Chelenza, whose recent triumph in battle has made him a favourite. Carlos returns in glory, and his choice of Elena as wife is duly enforced by the king. Very soon he goes back, reluctantly, to the battlefield to quell a rebellion in Calabria but first he speaks of his ailing marriage to the king, who promises to guard his honour. After witnessing Elena and César's clandestine meetings, the king warns the couple but is eventually driven to kill César. Carlos returns in time to hear César's offstage murder and to kill Elena himself.[13] As Charles Forker shows (p. liv), the resemblances to *The Cardinal* are few; the heroine prefers a court gallant to the soldier for whom she is intended and whose fiery honour resents that preference; she tries to deceive the soldier; and she receives a letter from him. Forker argues that the catastrophes are quite differently managed and that the Cardinal has no equivalent in *El buen vecino*. More importantly, he contrasts the plays' moral systems. In *The Cardinal* everyone deplores Alvarez's murder, whereas César and Elena appear as victims of a just vengeance. There is further evidence on both sides. Elena's 'no temas al Rey ni al mundo' (p. 1)[14] resembles Rosaura's confident despatching of a timid Alvarez to the garden while she confronts the Cardinal (II.iii.66–9); Elena, like Rosaura, considers the possibility of her hated lover's death (p. 24, I.ii.223–5); César and Alvarez both seem weak-willed men. But the differences pile up. Carlos is a former lover ('antiguo amante', p. 1) and becomes Elena's husband; Columbo has never been loved by the Duchess and kills her husband. Although both women attempt to deceive, their plots are not comparable. Elena and César plan adultery while Carlos is away; Rosaura tricks Columbo into releasing her from her engagement, and does not confide in Alvarez. The letters sent to the heroines are similar in being letters from a soldier but Rosaura's brings freedom whereas Elena's describes her husband's anxieties about his marriage. Furthermore, the different morality enforces a different structure. In *El buen vecino*, the murders form the climax and are followed only by Carlos's remarriage, to Lucrecia. In *The Cardinal*, Alvarez's murder occurs half-way through the play and sets off a sequence of revenge and counter-revenge. I cannot believe that *El buen vecino* was in any sense a main source.

Fredson Bowers finds a possible precedent for the Cardinal's decision to rape and then murder Rosaura in *Sicily and Naples*, Samuel Harding's unacted tragedy, which was published in 1640.[15] Forker reinforces the suggestion (p. lv), instancing Harding's background of warfare, devious plans for revenge, his heroine's distracted mind, and her fear of being poisoned by the king's Machiavellian favourite. There are other small similarities. King Ferrando's 'stragling senses' (p. 7) anticipate Rosaura's 'straggling sense' (V.iii.197); the king's niece, Charintha, is 'soft as the Turtle' (p. 30) as is Rosaura (V.i,44); Charintha's lover, like Alvarez, compares his own low birth with his mistress's nobility (p. 29, I.ii.183ff.); both plays allude to the king's divinity (p. 46, II.iii.30).[16] If Shirley had recently read *Sicily and Naples* a few details might indeed have remained in his mind but then Shirley was influenced in this way by many, many plays.

There are stronger links with another play published in 1640, *The Rebellion*, by Thomas Rawlins. Here too there is a background of war, a heroine in love with a man who seems low-born, a devious villain, and also similar plot-devices. In both plays there is a council of war in II.i. In *The Rebellion*, Antonio, who wants a truce since the enemy is strong, is accused by the governor and by Machvile of being a coward and a traitor. The others present support Antonio. The incident resembles Columbo's quarrel with Hernando. At the end of *The Rebellion*, the dying Machvile feigns repentance, thereby gaining an opportunity to stab Antonio. The Cardinal also achieves his revenge through pretended remorse. Both plays contain a scene in which lesser characters prepare a play.[17] It is arguable that Rawlins's play was more influential than Harding's when Shirley planned and wrote *The Cardinal*.

Inevitably the play recalls Jacobean revenge tragedies. Most of *The Cardinal*'s editors mention Webster and *The Duchess of Malfi*, and Forker adduces parallels in plot, character and style.[18] Yet it is misleading to treat Shirley's play as a late and inferior version of

Webster's. In plot and character especially, the likenesses are fleeting. Rosaura, quite unlike the earlier duchess, is threatened by her prospective husband whose uncle, the Cardinal, is central to the play's action as Webster's cardinal is not. Forker parallels Hernando with Bosola 'in terms of general function' (p. xlix), but they are very different; he instances the name Antonio, but this is a common Spanish or Italian name often used by Shirley, and again the characters have quite different roles. Some of Forker's verbal links are more persuasive but then Shirley, who was a literary magpie, might well echo such a well-known play without taking the plot as his model.[19] If any revenge play foreshadows *The Cardinal* in plot the obvious candidate is *The Spanish Tragedy*. In Kyd's play the heroine loves a man who is not her family's choice; there too she is betrothed to his murderer; there too a woman declares she will exact vengeance; there too an admirer and friend of her lover opposes the murderer and is offered the heroine's love. Kyd's Balthazar, like Columbo, is a relatively honourable man who is accompanied by a more sinister villain; Kyd's king is easily swayed. And if shared names are to be invoked, both *The Cardinal* and the additions to *The Spanish Tragedy* include Pedro and Jaques among the servants. Again the parallels are incomplete. Horatio and Bel-Imperia forget vengeance in their sexual attraction, and Horatio is murdered before planning revenge.[20] Yet in plot *The Cardinal* is closer to *The Spanish Tragedy* than to *The Duchess of Malfi*. There do not however seem to be any verbal echoes, apart from the sharing of such common images as that of a ship in a storm.

The sources suggested bear out R. S. Forsythe's description of Shirley as unoriginal in his materials but original in his organisation of those materials (p. 149). No play appears to be the single source of *The Cardinal*'s action. Plot-devices come from the obscurest and from the greatest of Shirley's predecessors. He was a literary playwright whose plays bulge with memories of other men's words and of his own, with incidents and characters drawn, like the masque properties of III.ii, from stock.[21] Yet it has been argued that for the name character of this play we should look to contemporary politics. Forker follows F. S. Boas in suspecting allusions to Archbishop Laud, and develops the comparison between Shirley's villain and Charles's unpopular adviser. He cites attacks on Laud which resemble Rosaura's tirade against the Cardinal (II.iii.139–68); he outlines Laud's character and activities, and explains why Shirley, a firm loyalist, might criticise the archbishop.[22] It is difficult not to see some reflection of Caroline politics in Shirley's portrayal of an absolutist king dependent on a powerful adviser. Not only was Laud regularly accused of popery but the prologue's allusion to Richelieu (ll. 2–3) could have turned men's thoughts, even in court circles, to Laud, who had already been compared with Richelieu. In 1635, Sir Thomas Roe wrote about the archbishop to Elizabeth of Bohemia: 'Being now so great he cannot be eminent and show it to the world by treading in beaten paths and the exploded steps of others. But he must choose and make new ways, to show he knows and can do more than others; and this only hath made the Cardinal Richelieu so glorious.' He then urges Elizabeth to show Laud 'the way to make himself the Richelieu of England', by helping her.[23] The King of Navarre, threatened by an uprising in Aragon, can be roughly paralleled with Charles, menaced by the Scots in 1641, although Shirley's king, unlike Charles, easily defeats the invaders. And in the month before *The Cardinal* appeared on stage the Irish rebelled. Furthermore Rosaura's use of 'the short-haired men' as bogeymen enforces contemporary application, and Laud's presence would help to explain the play's lurking references to treason and to give contours to the Cardinal's rather nebulous aura of corruption.

The link should not be overstressed. *The Cardinal* is not primarily a political play. It would in any case have been too late to provide a warning against Laud, who was already imprisoned in the Tower—although earlier the suspicion of an attack on someone so influential could not have escaped the censure of the Master of the Revels. And besides the resemblance to Laud, this Cardinal has a good deal of the wicked adviser and unscrupulous favourite found in earlier plays, and repeatedly in Shirley's own.[24] The mixture of topical reference and stock character suggests that Shirley again blends his sources, drawing on Laud for some of the Cardinal's characteristics but not focusing on the archbishop. Although *The Cardinal* is not without political theory,[25] the play's ultimate emphasis is not on constitutional matters but on individuals engaged in a conflict which, despite their exalted status, is essentially domestic. The villain's crime is not the oppression and pillage of a nation but the murder and attempted rape of his ward.

Besides possible literary and historical sources, a strong influence on Shirley was his audience. Clifford Leech judges the theatre's patrons as partly responsible for drama's decline during Charles's reign. He characterises the Caroline audience as genteel, unreceptive of ideas, and disliking difficulty, especially in verse.[26] Shirley's prologue to *The Imposture*, licensed a year before *The Cardinal*, glories in emasculation:

> To the ladies, one
> Address from the author, and the Prologue's done:—
> In all his poems you have been his care,
> Nor shall you need to wrinkle now that fair
> Smooth alabaster of your brow; no fright
> Shall strike chaste ears, or dye the harmless white
> Of any cheek with blushes: by this pen,
> No innocence shall bleed in any scene.   (V, 181)

The prospect is uninviting. Prologues of the period demonstrate that the Caroline audience was vociferous in its criticism, and only the most stubborn—or financially independent—dramatist would be likely to stand firm against its values. *The Imposture*'s prologue begins by confessing Shirley's anxiety about the play's reception by its 'judges'. Michael Neill thinks that the willingness to criticise indicates a rather different audience from Leech's collection of genteel dummies. He claims that its members were highly sophisticated, a leisured class which emulated courtiers and their accomplishments. They enjoyed and evaluated plays. In response, the dramatists became more self-conscious and tried to appeal to the mind.[27] We know that Caroline theatre-goers were not all fools. Sir Humphrey Mildmay shows his discrimination in a liking for 'that rare playe', *The Lady of Pleasure*, and Abraham Wright combines his enjoyment of Shirley with brief critical analyses. He prefers an elaborate plot. *The Grateful Servant* is 'well contrived' whereas *The Bird in a Cage* is 'indifferent' because the plot, although new, is not intricate. Yet plot is not all. *Hyde Park* is let down by 'ordinary' lines, and *The Lady of Pleasure* is praised for its style despite a plot which fails to please. In play after play Wright adjudicates on plot and lines, criteria which show that his pleasure in the theatre was more intellectual than emotional.[28]

Leech implies that the language of Caroline dramatists is plain and straightforward because the audience was inattentive to complexities of sound. Neill explains things differently. He thinks that Caroline dramatists taught their audience to appreciate clear pure language.[29] The plain style had long been extolled but not always adopted, especially in drama where high emotion was frequently accompanied by elaborately figurative language. Marston attacks verbal extravagance but himself resorts to rant; other Jacobeans, especially

Webster and Tourneur, are far from plain. Shirley however writes
without much decoration. His plays include occasional overblown
speeches but his writing is notable for being, as he promises in the
prologue to *The Brothers*, 'clearly understood' (I, 191).[30] His style
might well suit an audience which preferred not to think too hard,
but his plainness could appeal equally to the cognoscenti for whom
plainness was intellectually popular.

III. THE PLAY

Wright's stress on the plots and lines of plays tells us what a Caroline
spectator might look for in *The Cardinal*. In his prologue, Shirley
gives primacy to the action: 'A poet's art is to lead on your thought /
Through subtle paths and workings of a plot' (ll. 7–8).[31] With a nice
touch of self-conscious humour he shares his opinion with the comic
servant who criticises the Duchess's wedding play: 'Under the rose,
and would this cloth of silver doublet might never come off again, if
there be any more plot than you see in the back of my hand'
(III.ii.44–6). It is as a craftsman that Shirley is most likely to be
praised by later critics: he is 'competent and estimable' in tragedy,
excellent in exposition.[32] Swinburne, even in censorious mood, finds
him achieving at worst 'passable craftsmanship and humble merit'.[33]
Yet Bas, Shirley's most recent biographer, chooses to condemn the
importance of plot: *The Cardinal*'s formal economy is linked with
superficiality (p. 188); 'personnages et idées sont sacrifiés à l'action
pure' (p. 200); the interest is in what happens, rather than in why it
happens (p. 426).[34] We tend now to devalue—even to avoid —coherent and capable plotting and yet in a literary world which included
Rawlins and Harding it is not to be sneered at. And 'what happens' is
not in this play entirely a shallow matter.

Shirley's last tragedy is a revenge play shorn of many of the
macabre accretions of the Jacobean imagination: no skulls, no poisoned helmets or pictures, no exulting in horrible deaths. With
unJacobean simplicity, *The Cardinal* presents a series of events culminating in a murder which is followed by the execution of revenge
on the murderer and his patron by their weaker opponents. For the
action, Swinburne has undiluted praise: 'a model of composition,
simple and lucid and thoroughly well sustained in its progress towards a catastrophe remarkable for tragic originality and power of
invention'.[35] There is little digression but much commentary. Scenes
in which the action progresses alternate with recapitulation of salient

facts; characters freely discuss the past deeds of others and their own intentions. Two anonymous lords and the Duchess's secretary, Antonio, talk about the Duchess Rosaura and her relationship to Columbo and Count D'Alvarez, whose warlike and courtly natures they contrast. They mutter about the Cardinal's power and are interrupted by news of invasion. After this exposition the Duchess appears in the melancholy mood already described, and her ladies, Valeria and Celinda, repeat the distinction between Columbo and Alvarez. Again news comes of the impending war, and with it the first movement onwards—Columbo will be general in the war, and the Duchess hopes for his death. Columbo's farewell and departure to the front advance the action, but in the main his and Alvarez's interviews with the Duchess recall and expand their antithetical characters. In the act's last moments, the Duchess hints at a plan for persuading Columbo to release her.

Act I is largely talk. The Duchess's quandary is clear, the action minimal. Act II moves rapidly as Rosaura bestirs herself. She writes to Columbo. She receives a reply and when she takes this to the king we learn that Columbo has set her free. She then claims Alvarez, her more attractive suitor, for a husband. Some significant events prepare for later action. At a council of war, Columbo falls out with one of his colonels, Hernando, and dismisses him. The Cardinal is an unwelcome visitor to the Duchess. They round on each other and eventually the Cardinal, left alone, promises revenge. The play's main battle-lines are drawn up. Yet in the midst of this act's developments, two colonels and two captains repeat what we already know about the Duchess and Columbo (II.i.139–50). If the interest lies in what happens, there is still time to anticipate and recapitulate.

In Act III, the courtiers continue to gossip about recent events. We hear of Columbo's victory and while we wait for his return, the Duchess's servants talkatively prepare a play. Then, during the more formal masque which the Duchess has chosen, Alvarez is murdered by Columbo. Again narrative takes over while Columbo tells the court about the Duchess's letter which, as we must have guessed, requested freedom. With Columbo's arrest the action could be complete, but in the interval between Acts III and IV the king pardons Columbo. We are not told how this has come about, although the Cardinal is manifestly responsible. What matters is that Columbo is free and that honest men react with wonder and horror. Act IV resembles Act I in pattern.[36] Hernando and two lords discuss the Duchess, the Cardinal, and Columbo. Shortly afterwards the

Duchess again displays a grief which has already been reported, and again receives contrasting visitors, one unwelcome, one welcome. The wrathful Columbo is this time followed by Hernando, who offers pity and help and is, like Alvarez, promised the Duchess's love. Further action is anticipated: Rosaura and Hernando plot the deaths of their opponents, and the Duchess decides to disarm suspicion by feigning madness. Very soon Hernando kills Columbo.

The gossiping lords introduce the last act; they tell us what we know already and a little that we do not know. Now an earlier side-issue, Celinda's bawdy talk, becomes relevant. A series of scenes shows us Antonio and Antonelli stalking Celinda. In such an atmosphere the Cardinal's plan to rape the Duchess before murdering her seems less extraordinary. She has after all been linked with four men—Mendoza, Columbo, Alvarez and Hernando—although Shirley does not mention her sexual allure before the last scene. Hernando's return to court leads to the Cardinal's expected death. His repentance and confession that he has poisoned the Duchess are plausible, for Shirley's wicked characters often repent,[37] and he had earlier planned to poison Rosaura (V.i.92). His offer to save her parallels—ominously—Edmund's dying reparation in *King Lear*. The antidote which he provides and drinks himself is one of intrigue drama's drugs of convenience. But in the end there is a sting. The remorse is feigned, the antidote a poison, the Duchess a dead woman. The Cardinal's wounds are pronounced 'not fatal' so that he can be hoist with his own petard. In truth, the audience cannot have been much surprised. The revenge tradition was by 1641 too familiar for Rosaura's death to come as a shock. Yet the delayed poisoning of the Duchess is still an effective final stroke.[38] In Shirley's previous tragedy, *The Imposture*, the innocent had survived.

I have dwelt on the plot not simply because Shirley himself considered a play's action important but because it illustrates his customary lucidity and one source of that lucidity—the repeating and discussing of information. There are however some local defects. The major plot weakness is the Duchess's letter to Columbo. She gambles either on his death in battle or on his complaisance, and she is easily exposed. We are too aware that, as Columbo guesses, ''Tis a device' (II.i.128).[39] I am not so sure that the hiatus between Acts III and IV is a failing: Bas thinks we should witness how the Cardinal engineers Columbo's release (p. 206). Yet we know the Cardinal can sway the king. That he can sway him in such a serious matter is 'wondrous' but since the focus is on the king's failure of justice it is appropriate that we should share the courtiers' astonishment without hearing the debate which explains away the king's strange decision. We do see what happens without quite seeing why but the effect is not necessarily weak. A further objection comes from Boas. The plot demands a change in the Cardinal's character; at first merely a cunning intriguer, he becomes in the last act a monster who plans rape and murder.[40] But it is only when Columbo dies that the Cardinal is encumbered with the task of revenge, and his capacity for evil has been indicated by an almost universal mistrust and the Duchess's direct accusations. The flaw lies rather in his sketchily drawn revenge plot. Shirley does not make it clear whether the visit from the court coquette, Celinda, is what makes him think of rape. In his soliloquy after her departure (V.i.86–99) the Cardinal reveals what he has decided but not how he has come to his decision. And we do not learn whether Celinda is, as Bas assumes (p. 188), the Cardinal's accomplice. In V.ii she draws off Antonio, leaving the Duchess without her usual male protector, but Shirley does not suggest that the Cardinal has put her up to it. The ending too is marred, this time by careful morality. After the Cardinal has confessed to poisoning Rosaura and has produced his antidote, the Duchess unexpectedly confesses:

> And must I owe my life to him whose death
> Was my ambition? Take this free acknowledgement,
> I had intent this night with my own hand
> To be Alvarez' justicer. (V.iii.243–6)

The only reason she owes her life to anyone is because the Cardinal has poisoned her—or so everyone believes. Hers is an oversensitive conscience, given to her so that she also can admit to a kind of guilt, and we can acquiesce more willingly in her death.[41] Shirley provides the guilty avenger required by revenge tragedy, thereby stretching probability to accommodate what is expected. Yet whatever its deficiencies, the plot of *The Cardinal* moves clearly and directly to its end, without the convolutions of some of its predecessors.

Shirley, like Wright, felt strongly about 'lines'. Apart from his remarks in the prologue of *The Brothers*, he frequently allows one character to tax another with obscurity: 'your language/ Is not so clear as it was wont' (*The Traitor*, I.i; II, 100); 'your language,/ . . . is dark and mystical' (*The Gamester*, II.iii; III, 221); 'I know not how to interpret, sir, your language' (*The Opportunity*, IV.i; III, 419). Plain language is often set against the rhetoric of a devious court:

> you talk too fine a language
> For me to understand; we are far from court,

> Where, though you may speak truth, you clothe it with
> Such trim and gay apparel, we, that only
> Know her in plainness and simplicity,
> Cannot tell how to trust our ears, or know
> When men dissemble.   (*The Sisters*, II.ii; V, 377)

In liking plainness and clarity, Shirley was at one with his times. The sixteenth-century abuse of style with elaborate tropes and figures—which Gabriel Harvey had called 'curls and curling-irons'—had been remedied by returning to the 'perspicuitie' advocated by Ben Jonson and many others.[42] It was for simplicity, clarity and elegance that Shirley's contemporaries praised him.[43]

Modern critics who, unlike Shirley's contemporaries, are not implicitly congratulating themselves on having struggled free of the previous century's stylistic tangles, are less impressed by a style whose major virtue is clarity.[44] Juliet McGrath thinks Shirley's distrust of verbal artifice explains why his plays lack 'linguistic vitality and variety'. She finds in his 'stress on clear, concrete language' the cause of his alleged shallowness: 'his emphasis on the limitations of language renders him unable either to define intellectual depth in character or to indicate consistently the conceptual motivation behind action'.[45] Bas, in a detailed account of Shirley's writing finds worse faults. He demolishes the dramatist's style, accusing it of 'paresse et . . . pauvreté' (p. 376), and singles out *The Cardinal* for its second-hand imagery (p. 383). If, like Bas, we pick phrases or sentences out of *The Cardinal* and assess the sprightliness of the English we may agree with him, but if we look at speeches in context, and the play in its social and linguistic setting, we understand some of the reasons for that 'pauvreté'. And we begin to see that this play is not simply the last Jacobean revenge play: its style is part of a difference which sets it apart from its predecessors.

The basic style of *The Cardinal* is clear but stiff. Shirley is likely to use verb-noun phrases where an honest verb would be less stodgy. Alvarez fears that "'Tis not a name that makes / Our separation' (I.ii.208–9), although 'separates us' would express his fear more vividly and reduce our impression that his lines have been written for him. Perhaps in contrast, the first colonel's 'While we have tameness to expect' (II.i.25) fits what it says, but shortly afterwards keenness is unforgivably blunted: 'The men are forward in their arms, and take / The use with avarice of fame' (II.i.34–5). The Duchess instead of seeming disturbed 'expressed a trouble' (II.i.126); the Cardinal will 'perform a visit' (II.ii.1). Often these phrases depend on a neutral verb—'make', 'have', 'take', 'express', 'perform', words which contribute nothing to the life of a passage and make the lines seem static. Even verbs of motion or anticipation, such as 'advance' or 'expect', lose their impetus through over-use in phrases. Sometimes the vocabulary is not only predictable but careless. Shirley's ear seems deaf to repetitions. During the play preparations both a servant and the scenery for a masque are troublesome (III.ii.13 and 36). The Duchess's 'Expect me in the garden' (I.ii.150) is awkwardly picked up in 'This is above all expectation happy' (I.ii.151).

The repetitions sound casual, as if Shirley has a particular word fixed in his head for a while. The stiff and formal language is a different matter. The language of a play, more than that of a novel or a poem, needs to be considered not just in the context of literary language, but in terms of the language used by its audience. At the beginning of the century Sir William Cornwallis complained about his countrymen's false eloquence, and fabricated as an instance, 'O *Signiour*, the starre that governs my life in contentment give me leave to interre my selfe in your armes.'[46] And the complaints continued. Over fifty years later Dorothy Osborne told of a servant who believed 'putting pen to paper was much better then plaine writing'.[47] Jacobean and Caroline letter-writing preserves, amongst much that is refreshingly direct and colloquial, a more pretentious style. Dr John Bowle, seeking preferment from the Marquis of Buckingham, 'could not by any level taken frome my poore indeavors have measured the favor which your Honor graced mee withall'. 'I am embowldened to entreat yow to doe me soe much favour as to take some . . . oportunety' wrote the Earl of Cork to Sir Edmund Verney. Edward Peyton offered up a letter to his sister, Mrs Anne Oxinden, 'at the alter of your clemency', and Sir Simonds D'Ewes wrote to Sir Henry Willoughby 'to implore your favour in vouchsafing mee liberty' to 'addresse . . . affection' to his daughter.[48]

Several of these examples illustrate the fondness for replacing a verb with a weaker verb and noun. Yet the last few are from letters whereas Shirley's characters *talk* in stiff phrases. There is plenty of evidence that social climbers in seventeenth-century England were taught not just to write but to speak formally. The letter-writing textbooks of the late sixteenth and early seventeenth centuries were accompanied by conversation manuals. Benvenuto Italian's *The Passenger* was published in 1612. It provides model dialogues in parallel English and Italian texts. 'Doe me the favour', the courteous Alatheus asks his friend, 'to accept of my intentive desire to serve you' (p. 371). Eutrapelus is stricken with nouns: 'the debility of my condition should indeede rather reverence you with a divote silence, then in an outward demonstration of words' (p. 389). More nearly contemporary with *The Cardinal* is *The Academy of Complements*[49] which presents as suitable address to a great lord, 'it will be an addition unto my felicity, if I may approve this present opportunity, to make tender of my service' (p. 61); a lady is begged 'to excuse my audacity, and to pardon my temerity' (p. 77). Nouns proliferate.

Seventeenth-century comments about bombastic style; the more formal passages of upper-class letters; conversation manuals; these all suggest that a stodgy diction, overendowed with nouns, and with phrases instead of single-word verbs, was associated with courtly and polite society and aspired to by its imitators. Compliments were readily linked with the court.[50] As my examples show, this formal style was not unique to the Caroline period, but there does seem to be an upsurge of critical concentration on compliment in the 1620's, notably in Shirley's own first play, *Love Tricks* (1625), in Thomas Randolph's *The Drinking Academy* (?1626), and in some of Ford's plays. The trouble with *The Cardinal* is that it reflects, without criticising, the formal mode of genteel Englishmen of the time.[51] Some of their favourite words are in the play—'protestation', 'vouchsafe', 'oblige', 'commend'. What is worse, Bas argues that the play contains some of Shirley's most persistently stiff and flat writing. But if we turn to *The Cardinal* we shall have to modify the impression that Shirley wrote unthinkingly in the bland manner of cultivated Englishmen.

Extended wordy stretches occur in formal passages, such as the exchange between Alvarez and the king (II.iii.17–29), which the king ends with a promise, not to 'recompense' Alvarez but to 'find / A compensation'. IV.i includes a stiff little conversation between king and Cardinal:

> *King.* Commend us to the Duchess, and employ
>   What language you think fit and powerful,
>   To reconcile her to some peace. My lords.
> *Cardinal.* Sir, I possess all for your sacred uses.   (ll. 51–4)

Here are three main features of the bland style: fashionable vocabulary—'commend'; a phrase for a verb—'employ / ... language'; and meaningless compliment in the Cardinal's line. Such diction prevails in *The Cardinal* because there is so much courtly conversation. But the play is not uniformly written in this public

mode.[52] The formal language provides a base from which rise heightened passages. When the characters are disturbed or move into action, either the writing becomes livelier and more figurative or words
are pared right down. The most vivid passages come in several of
Hernando's speeches, in the Duchess's attack on the Cardinal where
she accuses him of winding courtiers' tongues 'Like clocks, to strike
at the just hour you please' (II.iii.151), and in Antonio's delight when
the vengeful Hernando arrives:

> I would this soldier had the Cardinal
> Upon a promontory, with what a spring
> The churchman would leap down; it were a spectacle
> Most rare to see him topple from the precipice,
> And souse in the salt water with a noise
> To stun the fishes; and if he fell into
> A net, what wonder would the simple sea-gulls
> Have, to draw up the o'ergrown lobster,
> So ready boiled! He shall have my good wishes.   (V.ii.105–13)

The formal base is still there—'what wonder ... / Have'—but it is
overlaid with lively imagery and strong verbs: 'leap', 'topple',
'souse', 'stun'.

At the other extreme, Shirley's narrative manner is an efficient
vehicle for the action. Here his main aim is to subordinate words to
facts, and so his style features compact grammatical devices. In
Columbo's description of how he was deceived, zeugma, ellipsis and
apposition all help to compress information:

> Read there how you were cozened, sir,
> Your power affronted, and my faith, her smiles
> A juggling witchcraft.   (III.ii.133–5)

Parenthesis adds a vital detail in the following passage:

> I sent
> That paper, which her wickedness, not justice,
> Applied, what I meant trial, her divorce.   (III.ii.163–65)

The Act I exposition is concise; only 'Alas poor lady' breaks into the
initial parade of facts. Moreover, although the first lord's ignorance is
artificial, the first scene of the play seems a model of normal conversation when set against the efforts of some of Shirley's contemporaries. There is none of the larding with 'Thou knowest' and 'it is true'
which encumbers the opening lines of Carlell's *The Deserving
Favourite* (between 1622 and 1629); and in nineteen lines Shirley
summarises relationships more complex than his fellow professional

Glapthorne describes in the sixty lines of bombast which open *Argalus and Parthenia* (between 1632 and 1638). At the very least Shirley's writing is a craft of which many Caroline dramatists, amateur and professional, knew little.

Shirley also cuts words away in a crisis. Alvarez's murderers act in silence. They enter as masquers and summon their victim; meanwhile a brief conversation among the watchers threatens danger.

> *King.* Do you know the masquers, madam?
> *Duchess.*   Not I, sir.
> *Cardinal.* [*Aside*] There's one, but that my nephew is abroad,
>   And has more soul than thus to jig upon
>   Their hymeneal night, I should suspect
>   'Twere he.   (III.ii.87–91)

'Has . . . soul', another grouping of neutral verb and noun, is countered by the jolliness of 'jig'. The climax which follows is largely visual. Columbo and the masquers '*bring in* ALVAREZ *dead*' and when the king asks where he is, '*Columbo points to the body*.' The onlookers react at first with questions and exclamations, keeping words to a minimum. Language here is unobtrusive, so that the spectator concentrates on what he sees.

If the wordy style of which Bas complains is never far away, it is accompanied both by a simpler narrative manner and by a more vigorous, figurative diction. Occasionally however the heightened passages may seem overstated. In Act II, Rosaura receives Columbo's reply to her letter. Antonio's description of Columbo's angry response to the Duchess's message (II.ii.28–33) teases Rosaura, creating a spurious excitement. He motivates, but does not entirely justify the *frisson* of horror in her reaction:

> My soul doth bathe itself in a cold dew;
> Imagine I am opening of a tomb,   [*Opens the letter.*]
> Thus I throw off the marble to discover
> What antic posture death presents in this
> Pale monument to fright me—   (II.ii.39–43)

Columbo has released the Duchess. The extended imagery of death and the tomb creates an atmosphere of imminent and real disaster and seems gratuitously melodramatic, but with hindsight we may find it has prepared us for Columbo's menace and the death he brings. Similar imagery features in Hernando's soliloquy before the denouement (V.iii.56–83). Since Hernando, concealed in the Duchess's chamber, expects the Cardinal's entry and a chance for vengeance, images of death—hearse-cloth, mourners, ashes, ghost—are not inconsistent with events. The speech modulates successfully between Hernando's thoughts and his feelings and has a strong emotional unity which overcomes the stock diction.[53]

In general, Bas is right about Shirley's style. His commitment to the noun and to inert verbs results in a rather static verse. But Bas's selective method gives a flatter impression of Shirley's style than the dramatist deserves. If we attend to speaker and occasion we meet a variety of modes appropriate to the events of the plot. We are also driven to consider larger issues of tone. In this play a remarkable amount of the dialogue is talk by courtiers and about courtiers. Whereas the Jacobeans—in particular Webster—presented abnormal events taking place in a diseased and abnormal society, Shirley depicts an ordered court peopled in the main by well-intentioned, morally sane, if rather passive characters. Forker accuses the court of 'vacillation and polite cynicism' (p. lxvii) but his judgement ignores the attitudes of the two lords and the loyalty of Placentia and of Antonio, whose questionable jokes are excused as a reaction to the depressing atmosphere of the Duchess's household and whose seduction by Celinda shows his lack of sophistication. The language reflects the difference between Shirley and most of the Jacobeans. Jonson believed that 'Wheresoever, manners, and fashions are corrupted, Language is' (*Wks.*, VIII, 593). Webster developed a vein of rich, dark, obsessive imagery for his rich, dark, obsessive characters. Shirley's society is not on the moral alert but neither is it especially corrupt and its speech is fittingly undynamic but clear, neither perverse nor inspired. There is however one strong Jacobean connection—with Beaumont and Fletcher. They also use everyday language and Fletcher in particular has a 'command of the courtier's conversation'.[54] Undoubtedly they anticipated and influenced Shirley's Caroline mode. Yet there is a difference of tone. Beaumont and Fletcher lay more stress than Shirley on evil and unnatural passions; they create with their 'emotional rhetoric' 'a world apart', a world of extremes.[55] Shirley's catastrophe erupts with unexpected horror into an ordinary world and it is because evil is not the norm that *what* happens is significant. It may not even be too rash to note that in contemporary England terrible and inconceivable events had begun to strike a comfortable and sophisticated court.

Shirley's skilful plotting has been generally acknowledged; his contemporaries praised his language and even his detractors admit its clarity. But his virtues in plot and style are closely related to his alleged defects. Character is at times a function of the plot; the plain style does not achieve the depth and complexity for which Shakespeare is admired. Shirley seems to be weak in just those areas where the great Elizabethans and Jacobeans are most powerful: characterisation, imagery and theme. The people are often types; the weak king, the villainous favourite, the blunt soldier, the courtier, the virtuous heroine—the latter frequently set against a lady of easier morals. The imagery is competently marshalled from the Jacobean store but does little to stir the mind or the emotions. Muriel Bradbrook complains that Shirley borrows 'the whole of the Revenge convention except that living core which was its justification, the imagery, the peculiar tone, the poetry'.[56] And as a revenge play *The Cardinal* is little more than an action. Shirley does not make us think about the morality of revenge or about its effect on the avengers. One of the harshest comments on this play comes from Clifford Leech who, after praising Shirley's competence, cites *The Cardinal* as an example of 'the nullity of Caroline tragedy'.[57]

If we accept all these negatives we are bound to consider *The Cardinal* not worth reading or seeing twice. Yet if again we look at what happens in this play, instead of treating it as an anaemic Jacobean tragedy, we may find more to interest us. Bowers argues that *The Cardinal* does consider the ethics of revenge (p. 231), but it is rather late in the revenge tradition to expect much further illumination of the morality of vengeance, an ambiguous topic even in its heyday. Shirley deploys the plot-motifs of revenge, the masque of death, the lustful villain, the devious poisoning, but despite its four avengers his play's themes and ideas have little to do with vengeance. Instead, Shirley touches on political issues. Current political thought was inevitably much occupied with monarchs and their advisers. One of the most powerful scenes in *The Cardinal* tackles the Cardinal's misuse of his authority. In Act II, scene iii, the Cardinal in disappointed rage attacks the Duchess and is in turn anatomised. Rosaura's denunciation is sincere and purposeful. She directs the Cardinal to begin his correction 'at home' and lists his villainies. An enemy of the people, a corrupter of the king and his court, he even injures the church he was installed to defend:

>   'tis your
> Ambition and scarlet sins that rob
> Her altar of the glory, and leave wounds
> Upon her brow; which fetches grief and paleness
> Into her cheeks; making her troubled bosom
> Pant with her groans, and shroud her holy blushes
> Within your reverend purples.   (ll. 157–63)

She begs him to reform 'before the short-haired men / Do crowd and call for justice' (ll. 167–8). The pressure of contemporary events reinforces the Duchess's pleading but her speeches already have a strength and eloquence which deepen the play's effect. For a moment her personal battle spreads to the world outside. Critics have found in Shirley a 'serious attitude toward life and ... severe morality',[58] and these speeches reveal a man deeply and movingly affected by wrong. Even the Cardinal, who has come to domineer, stays to applaud the Duchess's spirit.

Elsewhere Shirley draws attention to the king's role. Catherine Belsey has argued that 'in order to be a play about revenge, *The Cardinal* has to become a play about a crisis of justice'. The play is royalist, and presents the king as absolute, as the source of justice; he dominates in the key scenes (III.ii and the second half of V.iii) and cannot be considered a weak character since his behaviour is confident, his main speeches authoritative. The plot demands that his justice fail, since without Columbo's release there would be no need for revenge; Hernando undertakes a personal struggle for social justice in a world deserted by the divine justice which should have emanated from the king. Yet at the end of the play the king replaces Hernando as the dominant figure and blithely reminds us that kings must be on their guard. The action and the royalist theme are at odds.[59] I agree that the king is prominent in this play but I am not persuaded that plot confounds theme. The king's divine right is invoked in III.ii.108 and III.ii.196 although the second allusion is the Cardinal's and sounds like ironic flattery. If the king's power is absolute, his bent is conciliatory. The second lord's reaction to the Aragonian aggression is to wonder 'What have they, but the sweetness of the king, / To make a crime?' (I.i.62–3). When the king speaks to Hernando of the quarrel with Columbo he insists that 'we must have / You reconciled' (II.iii.1–2); he plans to compensate Alvarez for giving up Rosaura (II.iii.27–9); and he asks the Cardinal to forgive the Duchess: 'I heard you had a controversy with / The Duchess, I will have you friends' (III.i.49–50). Once Alvarez is dead, the king again sends the Cardinal to the Duchess 'To reconcile her to some peace' (IV.i.53). His initial reaction to the murderer is merciful:

> We thought to have put your victory and merits
> In balance with Alvarez' death, which while
> Our mercy was to judge, had been your safety. (III.ii.235–7)

He uses his authority, sensibly enough, to smooth over offences to others, but what he cannot ignore is an affront to himself. He may forgive Alvarez's murder but not 'the offence, / That with such boldness struck at me' (III.ii.207–8). Thus in his central speeches of judgement against Columbo, the king becomes syntactically both subject and object (III.ii.182–91, 200–205, 206–15, 235–40); he is both judge and victim. Forker accuses him of accepting evil 'with a rebuke to violated etiquette' (p. lxvii) but his reaction is not as morally frivolous as Forker's charge implies for, as Lawrence Stone explains (p. 232), physical attack at court was regarded as 'an exceptionally grave offence' since it could so easily put the monarch himself at risk. Columbo's imprisonment is for an assault on majesty, and thus his release is a defeat of the king's absolute authority, a defeat befitting a king whose favour is in his own words 'indulgence' (III.ii.209, V.iii.295). His final speech in the play once more centres on his own injury, not on the Duchess's death:

> How much are kings abused by those they take
> To royal grace! Whom, when they cherish most
> By nice indulgence, they do often arm
> Against themselves.   (V.iii.293–6)

Here there is an interesting pattern as kings move from the passive ('are kings abused') to the active mode ('they take', 'they cherish', 'they . . . arm') to suffering object ('Against themselves'). In this context the banal last line, '*None have more need of perspectives than kings*', becomes more relevant. Again the syntax makes its own point; the sentence is about kings but 'kings' is not unequivocally the grammatical subject. The absolutism is qualified, and for good reason. The king's misjudgements in enforcing the engagement to Columbo (III.ii.182–91), in freeing Columbo and in trusting the Cardinal as Rosaura's guardian precipitate the tragedy. He is indeed more important in this play than are the justicers in many earlier revenge plays, but his significance is not blurred by the plot. The central story is of the Duchess but she is destroyed because the king lacks 'perspectives'. Her fate illustrates on the private, personal level the political theme which informs the play, that of all people an absolute monarch cannot afford to be wrong.[60]

Such thematic material as *The Cardinal* contains has more to do with politics and justice than with revenge. Yet although the atmosphere is not that of the Jacobean revenge plays, there are some signs of a more disordered world which seem to belong to the darker settings of Shirley's predecessors. Not only does the play have a

background of military strife but there are warnings of treason. Early
in the play, the first lord remarks of the Aragonian offensive,

> This flame has breath at home to cherish it;
> There's treason in some hearts, whose faces are
> Smooth to the state.   (I.i.70–2)

We expect the treachery in court to have some link with the smooth
faces and plotting hearts of the main plot, but the hints are not taken
up, although treason, treachery and betrayal lurk in the play. The
Cardinal is believed to control spies (I.i.19–20). Columbo accuses
Hernando of being either a coward or a traitor (II.i.36–7), and the
accusation rankles. Hernando later tells the Duchess: 'If you will call
me coward, which is equal / To think I am a traitor, I forgive it'
(IV.ii.150–1). The Duchess suspects she may be betrayed
(IV.ii.144–5), and Hernando fears betrayal (V.ii.77, V.iii.123), but
both use the term in a weakened, personal sense. Treason is part of
the metaphoric structure which supports Shirley's plot.

It is not misleading to speak of a metaphoric structure since, despite the plainness and lack of poetic richness, Shirley uses his imagery thematically to point up the play's main oppositions and connec-
tions. Appropriately in a play which begins with the topics of love
and war, Shirley applies the standard comparison between them.
Columbo is first characterised as 'The darling of the war, whom
victory / Hath often courted' (I.i.23–4), Valeria remarks that 'war
and grim-/ Faced honour are his mistresses' (I.ii.55–6), and he himself thinks of kissing women as 'court tactics' (I.ii.107). Military
imagery accompanies him through the play, whereas the Duchess is
forced to play a passive role. Publicly she speaks of 'A peace con-
cluded 'twixt my grief and me', while privately regretting that 'I
must counterfeit a peace, when all / Within me is at mutiny' (I.ii.16
and 27–8). Even after planning revenge she pretends, to protect herself, that the Cardinal has given her 'sorrow so much truce'
(IV.ii.304).

There are many allusions to the bleeding wounds of love and war;
the strong characters actively inflict bloody wounds and their opponents bleed. For Alvarez, who protests that he 'would not shrink to
bleed / Out [his] warm stock of life' (II.iii.25–6), hyperbole becomes
fact. In contrast Columbo sheds blood, dealing out 'bloody execution' (III.ii.213); his soul 'is purpled o'er, and reeks with innocent
blood' (IV.ii.45). Relationship is defined in terms of blood
(II.iii.106) as too is rank (I.ii.201), and even the colour of blood is

significant. In the Cardinal's red-robed presence is figured the blood
which spills from his ambitious plans. There must be a strong tempt-
ation to any designer to exploit the play's dominant red and purple.[61]

The imagery enhances the play's emotional antitheses. The
Duchess's side stands for love and peace. There are metaphors of
growth: 'Now the king / Hath planted us, methinks we grow already'
(II.iii.60–1). A comparison may derive from religion—the Duchess's
fame 'stands upon an innocence as clear / As the devotions you pay to
heaven' (II.iii.117–18); or from natural beauty—the Duchess is
'Serene, as I / Have seen the morning rise upon the spring'
(II.i.117–18). Opposing the gentle vein are warfare and violence, the
spilling of blood, disease, fire, storm and devilry. Yet despite their
appeal to the feelings, the images ultimately have an intellectual
rather than an imaginative effect. The allusions to the devil, for instance, lack resonance. This is because the Cardinal, to whom they
usually apply (as at III.i.74 and V.iii.54), is a limited embodiment of
evil. 'Devil' tells us what to think of him, but his 'cloven foot'
(V.iii.165) does not chill us as does Iago's. The metaphorical world of
The Cardinal does not stretch our imaginations, nor does it provoke a
gut response to good and evil; it works as an aid to moral clarity,
providing a coherent figurative background to the plot and
characters.

The characters are, in many of Shirley's plays, his weakest point
but in *The Cardinal* we come across some unexpected variation.
Richard Gerber writes of a grand style being given to tiny people, of
villains who are villains in a small way.[62] Initially this criticism seems
true of the Cardinal. His pride is repeatedly stressed; he is disliked
and distrusted; but his prime aim in the early parts of the play is to
advance his family by marrying his nephew to a fortune. The complaints about his pride and villainy are inadequately borne out by his
actions, although his practice of lurking in the background when he
enters a room may substantiate the accusations of spying. When he
turns rapist and murderer, he is motivated by the straightforward
desire to avenge his nephew. Yet as he moves from venial plotting to
an intellectual pleasure in planning rape only to find himself sensu-
ally aroused by his own vengeance, we may detect once again this
play's atmosphere of disturbance and evil rising out of the ordinary.
The Cardinal's moment of lust contrasts with the mental control of a
man whose reaction to his nephew's crime is 'Now to come off were
brave' (III.ii.112), and who reacts in the same way to his own death:

now it would be rare,
If you but waft me with a little prayer,
My wings that flag may catch the wind.   (V.iii.279–81)

His main opponent seems for much of the play a firm character. The Duchess is burdened with our memories of the Duchess of Malfi and of Bel-Imperia but she has a considerable presence. She stage-manages her release by Columbo; she confronts the Cardinal boldly, sending a nervous Alvarez to wait in the garden; she turns the Cardinal's attention from her own follies by denouncing his crimes. Although her feigned madness alternating with apparently genuine insanity derives from Hamlet, Shirley gives it his own gentle, rather pretty stamp. But the plot works against the Duchess's characteris-ation. She who was so positive becomes passive, dependent on Hernando's help. The change is highlighted by the structural similarity between I.ii and IV.ii: in I.ii, the Duchess is in control during her interviews with Columbo and Alvarez; in IV.ii, she is weak and defeated. Columbo hectors her and Hernando takes over her task of revenge. Although the Cardinal grows in villainy he is matched with no mighty opposite, for as he begins to show his 'cloven foot' the Duchess, who had earlier displayed a spirit 'to tame the devil's' (II.iii.170), crumples. Her collapse removes tension from the central conflict. Yet the combination of submission and insis-tence on choosing her own husband is interesting. Three years after *The Cardinal*, Lady Anne Halkett began a struggle to be matched with the man of her choice but eventually, Stone records, 'made a practical prosaic match of the most traditional kind'. Stone regards her story as typical of the seventeenth century—a woman caught between the tradition of female submissiveness and new ideas of in-dependence and personal decision.[63] The Duchess is not unlike Anne Halkett.

The Duchess's choice in marriage is puzzling. Alvarez is a court-ier, a type often criticised by Shirley.[64] Columbo and the Cardinal make an issue of his courtliness. Columbo despises this 'curlèd minion' (III.ii.137), and the Cardinal compares the two suitors:

Because Alvarez has a softer cheek,
Can like a woman trim his wanton hair,
Spend half a day with looking in the glass
To find a posture to present himself,
And bring more effeminacy than man
Or honour to your bed; must he supplant him?   (II.iii.109–14)

Although prejudiced, these remarks must exaggerate the truth; they are unlikely to be a flat lie. Interestingly, the Restoration cast list preserved in the Leeds University copy of Octavo shows that in the early 1660s Alvarez was played by Kynaston shortly after that actor had given up the female roles for which he was famous. Less biased commentators also hint at Alvarez's weakness. The first lord praises his wisdom in not insisting on his prior claim to the Duchess, but the other lord is doubtful. Alvarez has 'tamely' renounced the Duchess (I.i.30): 'If wisdom, not inborn fear, make him compose, / I like it' (I.i.43–4). Alvarez confirms his suspicions. In his first interview with the Duchess, he outlines the dangers, from king, Cardinal, and Columbo, that confront himself and Rosaura. 'Then you do look on these with fear', she responds (I.ii.217). He protests that his concern is for her, but he does fear. In II.iii, he watches with trepidation the Cardinal's approach. 'Take no notice of his presence', advises the Duchess, 'Leave me to meet and answer it' (ll. 66–7). He obeys. She is the dominant partner in birth and personality. Here we *are* reminded of the Duchess of Malfi. Alvarez's submission and lack of eagerness to stand by her make us uneasy, especially when his offer to give her up to Columbo is preceded by thoughts of himself:

> I am a man on whom but late the king
> Has pleased to cast a beam, which was not meant
> To make me proud, but wisely to direct
> And light me to my safety. (I.ii.188–91)

The Duchess is not thinking of safety, nor later is Hernando, who leaves his 'own security' to avenge Alvarez (V.iii.67). Even Valeria's no doubt politic praise of Alvarez's sweet composition, speaking eyes and natural black curls (I.ii.37 and 39–42), accords with the Cardinal's criticism. So does Alvarez's speech. His first appearance is marked by impersonal compliment (I.ii.161–3) and a balanced and antithetical syntax redolent of courtliness and cautious premeditation (I.ii.167–71 and 177–9). He is an unusual choice for one of Shirley's heroines. Does Shirley here couple courtliness with timidity, and hint that the Duchess loves unworthily?

Consider the man she rejects. Columbo is a blunt soldier, a type favoured by Shirley, and often set to his advantage against a courtly foil. Shirley breaks down the usual associations by setting Columbo against Hernando, another soldier, as well as against Alvarez. At first he seems stock. Valeria's remark that 'His talk will fright a lady' (I.ii.55) promises someone resembling Beaumont and Fletcher's

Memnon in *The Mad Lover*, but when Columbo appears he breaks
that mould:

> Madam, he kisseth your white hand, that must
> Not surfeit in this happiness—and ladies,
> I take your smiles for my encouragement;
> I have not long to practise these court tactics.   (I.ii.104–7)

This is polished enough, with a touch of old-fashioned formality in
the inflected ending of 'kisseth'. Celinda admires his expert embrace.[65] Columbo is not a villain. The first lord praises him, finding
even his pride appropriate (I.i.23–7), and even after Alvarez's murder, the same lord is prepared to make excuses for Columbo
(IV.i.38–9). He has the stage soldier's hasty temper, as one of his own
colonels concedes (II.i.140), and yet he does not seem wholly unjus-
tified in attacking Hernando as a coward since Hernando's strategy is
to sit tight until the enemy eat and drink themselves into a stupor. His
summoning of a council of war implies deviousness since he already
knows of a plot to betray the city they are menacing and thus he needs
no advice. But the council is less a test of Columbo's supporters than
a device prompted by the plot's demand for a quarrel with Columbo
which will give Hernando a personal motive for revenge. In the same
scene Columbo's brusque 'No poetry' in response to Antonio's fanci-
ful description of the Duchess (II.i.117–20) is the kind of reaction
Shirley usually gives to favoured characters.

In the context of Shirley's attitudes to courtiers and soldiers,
Columbo and Alvarez reward scrutiny; the courtier plays the juv-
enile lead, the uncourtly soldier is a 'villain'. The contrast is not
thoroughly worked out. Alvarez is too empty to interest us for long,
Columbo is not a bad man. Yet there is just enough complexity,
intended or not, to make us wonder about the Duchess's judgement
in choosing Alvarez, and her justification for treating Columbo as she
does. His revenge becomes vindictive when he threatens to destroy
all future lovers but he has perhaps some grounds for his murderous
reaction against Alvarez. We do begin to question our assumptions
about avengers and their victims. Although Shirley does not concentrate our attention on the moral issues of revenge we are left with
some thinking to do.

The play which Shirley reckoned 'the best of my flock' (Dedication, l. 11) has ever since had a mixed reception. In 1671, Edward
Howard ranked it among 'the highest of our English Tragedies', but
a century later Charles Dibdin found it 'a very dull thing'. Praise of

The Cardinal is, on the whole, qualified: the play 'can hold its own
with any but the greatest masterpieces of that age' (Parrott and Ball);
it is 'a notable romantic tragedy' (Nason); in 'construction and acta-
bility' it is one of the best of the Elizabethan revenge plays (Bowers).
Schelling points to what may be the dramatist's main drawback when
he comments that Shirley has 'the shortcomings of the moderate
man'.[66] For *The Cardinal* could be seen as the work of a man too
much in control, perhaps even with too sane and untroubled a
mind.[67] Shirley is an elegant craftsman; a swift, well-organised plot
progresses with the help of a clear style, a competent varying of regis-
ter and a simple but coherent structure of imagery. Theme, characterisation and images lack the imaginative excitement of the
Jacobeans. Yet the ambiguous treatment of Rosaura's lovers and the
embryonic political themes of the play invite an intellectual response,
and our feelings as well as our minds are impressed by this representation of sudden disastrous events exploding in a relatively civilised
and well-behaved court. For all its Jacobean ingredients, *The
Cardinal* is a tragedy of its own times.

IV. ORIGINAL STAGING AND THEATRE HISTORY

Although we have no contemporary drawing or description of the
Blackfriars Theatre, enough detail of its location and dimensions is
revealed in legal documents for several recent researchers to have
evolved precise, if conflicting, ideas of the theatre's size and
structure.[68] The plays known to have been performed at Blackfriars
give us some evidence about the stage equipment.[69] *The Cardinal*,
like other Blackfriars plays, calls for relatively simple staging. The
entrances at the beginning of Act I indicate two doors in the back of
the stage; two lords enter 'at one door', Antonio 'at the other'. The
theatre could accommodate flights, and entrances through a trap-
door, but *The Cardinal* makes no use of such spectacle although the
servants discuss whether a masque complete with descending throne
would be preferable to their play. Hernando's eavesdropping in Act
V needs hangings for concealment, and the theatre's bell rouses the
court at the catastrophe. The play makes no special demands, though
T. J. King considers a tree necessary for the garden (p. 77). John
Freehafer argues that by 1635 the private theatres were occasionally
using perspective scenery but none of his evidence comes from
Shirley's plays.[70]

The simple staging is not primitive staging. The King's Men were a sophisticated company, used to performing at court, and their dramatist was the author of *The Triumph of Peace*, the most spectacular masque of the Caroline period. *The Cardinal* shows some signs of spectacle deliberately avoided. Alvarez is killed during a masque, but by masquers whose entertainment is rudimentary, who lead their prey offstage, and who return bearing his body. Instead of focusing on the murder, Shirley shows reactions to the murder. He does include an onstage duel and Hernando's rescue of the Duchess from rape but he stages the final deaths unflamboyantly. Neither the Cardinal nor the Duchess seems to suffer much from taking poison. Their deaths are rapid and quiet. There is no stage direction to describe Hernando's death and so we can only speculate about whether his is a quick suicide or a more spectacular struggle. Suicide seems not to be in character, and Hernando's reference to 'sport' (V.iii.181) echoes his pleasure in the duel (IV.iii.16). His opponents are the foppish Antonelli and the Cardinal's servants, whom we may expect to overwhelm him with numbers rather than spirited sword-play. Shirley does not always seize opportunities for display. Disaster comes swiftly and suddenly. The stagecraft, as does the language, presents a fairly normal world with brief intrusions of violence. Indeed for a dramatist whose main output was Fletcherian tragi-comedy the comparative calm of *The Cardinal*'s moments of crisis is notable.

The play's later stage history is patchy. The existence of an alternative prologue which, with its allusion to the court's sojourn in York, could not have belonged to the original performance, suggests a revival in 1642.[71] After the Restoration, *The Cardinal* seems to have been popular for a while, perhaps—G. E. Bentley suggests (V, 1087)—because of the actor Hart, who had earlier gained his reputation in the part of Rosaura. Sir Henry Herbert records a performance on 23 July 1662 by the King's Company.[72] The cast for this revival—or for the performance on 2 October 1662—may well be that recorded in the copy of Octavo held in the Brotherton Library at Leeds University; the list includes Theophilus Bird (Second Lord) who was dead by 1663, and Walter Clun (Antonio) who was murdered in 1664. Several of the cast were boy actors before 1642. Charles Hart now played Hernando, one of a long series of major roles which included Mosca, Hotspur, Brutus, and Othello, a part which he took over from Nicholas Burt (the Cardinal). Columbo was given to Michael Mohun, who was later to play Volpone, Face, and Iago; Alvarez was Edward Kynaston, who had recently graduated from female roles. William Wintershall, noted as a comedian, took the minor part of First Lord, and the remaining roles attributed went to less well-known actors: Blagden (King), Marmaduke Watson (Alphonso), Bateman (Antonelli). Shortly afterwards we hear from Pepys, for whom the play seems to have improved on acquaintance. On 2 October 1662 he was cool about *The Cardinal*: 'a tragedy I had never seen before, nor is there any great matter in it'. 24 August 1667 found him won over with the help of the acting: 'After dinner, we to a play and there saw *The Cardinall* at the King's House, wherewith I am mightily pleased; but above all with Becke Marshall.' And on 27 April 1668 his approval was unqualified: at the King's playhouse he 'saw most of *The Cardinall*, a good play'.[73]

The great gap that follows is interrupted by a play on which *The Cardinal* had a small influence, Sophia Lee's *Almeyda*, *Queen of Granada*, performed at the Theatre Royal in Drury Lane on 20 April 1796.[74] The advertisement tells us: 'The story of ALMEYDA is wholly a fiction; and the incident which produces the catastrophe the only one not my own.—The deep impression made on me, long since, by a similar denouement, in an old play of JAMES SHIRLEY's, determined me to apply it.'[75] There are hints of other ingredients from *The Cardinal*. The Moorish Almeyda, who has been hostage to the King of Castile and loves his son, is returned as heir to Granada on her father's death. She has to rejoin the Moors while her lover Alonzo is at war. Abdallah her uncle plans to force her to marry his son Orasmyn. Alonzo is captured while secretly visiting Almeyda and she, mistakenly believing him dead, runs mad. Abdallah tries to persuade her to abdicate but is led to confess his own crimes. When Almeyda then faints, Abdallah, pretending she is poisoned, sends for an antidote which he drinks first. Abdallah, unlike the Cardinal, has knowingly killed himself in destroying his victim.

There have been few twentieth-century productions. The New York Public Library holds a programme for a performance by senior students at the Feagin School of Drama and Radio, in November 1948. For four performances *The Cardinal* hit Fifth Avenue. More important is the 1970 production at Farnham's Castle Theatre, the predecessor of the Redgrave Theatre. Malcolm Griffiths's production of *The Cardinal* with Maev Alexander as the Duchess and Brendan Barry as the Cardinal roused conflicting reactions. At worst Shirley was described as a dramatist who wrote 'at the fag end of a blood-and-thunder tradition'; at best came claims that the play had 'the violence of Marlowe, the robustness of Jonson and the poetry of

Shakespeare'.[76] What the critics pitched on was the very element of spectacle which I have argued is played down; the duel, attempted rape, suicide and most notably the murder of Alvarez.[77] There are two reasons for such an emphasis. In the context of other revenge tragedies Shirley's seems subdued but as one play in a season of calmer productions it is bound to seem typically bloodthirsty. Also stage effect was accentuated by one major peculiarity of the production. Alvarez's death did not occur offstage. Instead, during the wedding entertainment, he was invited to stand in a magician's vanishing box. He did not vanish but was apparently electrocuted. Presumably this coup de théâtre was added because the play was felt not to be startling enough in its first catastrophe, but inevitably its inclusion affects not just one scene but the tone of the whole play. My own memory of this production is of an honest revival which did not quite test the play's own merits. It would have been interesting to see whether Shirley's central scene, with the emphasis less on the murder than on its aftermath, was strong enough in its original form.

The most recent appearance of *The Cardinal* is also the most unexpected. In January 1979, the Magic Theatre of San Francisco staged *The Red Snake* by Michael McLure, who updated 'a near-forgotten, unplayable late Renaissance play by James Shirley called *The Cardinal*.'[78] Michael McLure, John Lion the director, and Peter Coyote, who played the Cardinal, are all prominent in experimental and controversial theatre; the Magic Theatre Company specialises in new works, often by new dramatists. What did this group of modern talents do with *The Cardinal*? The play seems to have been pared to its plot. Cardinal, king, Duchess, Columbo and Alvarez (the last two shortened to Collum and Dalv)[79] are bound in the same basic relationships except that the play 'begins and ends with' the Cardinal's 'erotic advances on the equally calculating Duchess' who has 'a will to power that equals any of the men's' and 'a healthy, well-indulged sexual appetite'.[80] Modern slang is substituted for Shirley's dialogue, not with entire success. Bernard Weiner complains about the uneasy blend of styles: 'McLure's characters are often into spouting philosophy and poetic observations about love, death and everything in between, so that their constant descent into scatology seems forced, overworked and, on several occasions, ludicrous.'[81] The theatre's press release of 20 December 1978 suggests a stronger political and social intent than emerges from Shirley's play: *The Red Snake* 'examines the brutality and corruption of sex, religion, politics, money and war'. These themes were reinforced by the setting, de-

scribed by Weiner as an 'abstract icy cave' which gradually became
blood-stained, and the costumes, at first white, later black and red.
Although McLure fundamentally altered *The Cardinal* it says much
for Shirley's play that a modern dramatist could find himself so
'greatly attracted to Shirley's play' that it inspired a new direction in
his own writing.[82]

V. THE TEXT

The text of *The Cardinal* presents no major problems. There was one
early edition of the play, published with five others in an octavo
volume, *Six New Playes*, in 1653. The last play, *The Court Secret*,
also bears this date but the title-pages of *The Brothers*, *The Sisters*,
The Doubtful Heir, *The Imposture*, and *The Cardinal* are dated 1652.
These five were staged in London between 1640 and 1642. Only *The
Doubtful Heir* seems to have been performed earlier, in Dublin
around 1638, and *The Court Secret* was never acted. The title-pages
state that the plays have not been printed before.

Bibliographically the plays are separate units, and copies survive
of *The Cardinal* bound alone.[83] Its collation is straightforward:
Octavo, A-E8, F4; A1, title-page; A1v, blank; A2 (missigned A3)-
A2v, Dedication; A3, Prologue; A3v, Commendatory verses by
'Hall'; A4, blank; A4v, Persons; B1-F3, text; F3v, Epilogue; F4-4v,
'A Catalogue of the Authors Poems already Printed'. The evidence of
watermarks and running-titles suggests half-sheet imposition of A
and F.[84]

The Cardinal is a very finished piece of printing but the copy is
unlikely to have been the theatre's prompt-book. There are some
difficulties with characters' names. The worst of these comes in I.ii,
where Valeria and Celinda are assigned each other's speeches (ll.
134–46). There is a further problem with the servants' names in
III.ii, though this would cause little difficulty in the theatre since
they are firmly labelled by number.[85] The Valeria/Celinda confusion
would surely have been tidied up in a prompt-book, as would the
unrecorded exits (for instance, III.ii.32) and unspecific entrances
such as '*Enter Secretary and Servants*' (III.ii.0.1).[86] The detailed
directions for the masque and duel perhaps suggest an author
anxious that things should be done his way. The signs point to an
authorial manuscript. Since some of Shirley's plays have survived in
different stages of composition we have evidence that there could be a
further version or versions in between the dramatist's foul papers

and the theatre's manuscript. In one instance, *The Court Secret*, there exists a scribal transcript, entitled *Don Manuell*, of an early state of the text with additions whose handwriting closely resembles Shirley's.[87] A. P. Riemer presents less spectacular evidence of Shirley's revisions in an account of the surviving versions of *The Constant Maid*. Riemer believes that revision and addition were a habit with Shirley, and he comments that other plays 'seem to have been extensively revised'.[88] Although the copy for *The Cardinal* may have been Shirley's foul papers, the playwright's practice elsewhere and the relative tidiness of the text suggest that the printer could have received an intermediate transcript, either by a scribe or by the author himself.

Octavo's lineation furnishes some further clues about the manuscript. There are many short and long lines, especially in conversation. Sometimes there is obvious mislineation. If we look at the relationship between *Don Manuell* and the printed text of *The Court Secret* we gain some notion of Shirley's working practice. *Don Manuell* is much less regular in metre, and full of deletions and insertions which lead to further variation in line length. *The Court Secret* of 1653 shows Shirley revising substantially and regularising many, but by no means all, of the lines. The history of *The Court Secret* implies that Shirley wrote rapidly through several versions. In both the surviving stages of *The Court Secret* and in *The Cardinal*, he settles into iambic pentameters in the long speeches but seems to have written the conversational stretches without especial attention to metre and then to have revised. *The Cardinal* manuscript probably represents a later stage in Shirley's writing process than does *Don Manuell* and may have been similar in condition to *The Court Secret*'s eventual copy-text. It may well have been scribal, with additions and deletions causing some confusion, and not entirely regular. For instance, at IV.ii.269, where the proof-correction must have involved a second look at the manuscript, there is a long line. The difficulty is made worse by Shirley's failure—or his copyist's—to mark elisions conscientiously. Although many elisions are indicated, roughly the same number remain unmarked. This feature is also characteristic of *Don Manuell*.

Octavo's other problems do not affect the establishing of a text. The first concerns the printer. The six plays, as the title-pages repeatedly tell us, were printed for the booksellers Humphrey Robinson and Humphrey Moseley. Moseley had a close association with two printers, Thoman Warren and Thomas Wilson, who in-

conveniently did not always sign their handiwork.[89] W. W. Greg
states that *Six New Playes* was divided between them, and he is followed by Forker, the only modern editor to discuss the printers.[90]
Greg is right, but the relationship of the Warren plays is not altogether straightforward. The headpiece to *The Cardinal* can also be
found in Sir John Suckling, *Poems etc.*, printed by Warren in 1648 (p.
3). Although it resembles the headpieces used in *The Brothers* and
The Imposture, both printed by Wilson, it is observably different.
The Cardinal and *The Sisters* both share ornaments and ornamental
letters with books printed by Warren between 1647 and 1658.
Bibliographically they are very close. The distribution of broken letters and the spelling show that both were set up from the one type-
case and both had only one compositor—very probably the same man
for both plays. *The Doubtful Heir* is quite different and, in the context
of *Six New Playes*, it looks like a Wilson printing. Like Wilson's
three plays and unlike *The Cardinal* and *The Sisters* it has an ornamental letter at the opening of the dedication; it shares no ornaments
with the other two Warren plays but uses an acorn ornament as do the
Wilson plays; among many minor details is the use of a font whose U
is the same as that of Wilson's plays but not of Warren's. Yet *The
Doubtful Heir* was printed by Warren. All its ornaments appear in
books printed by Warren in 1652 or 1653, notably the ornamental
letters which begin the dedication and the text.[91] Warren organised
the printing of these plays less simply than Bas implies when he
speculates that the order in *Six New Playes* is the order of printing (p.
824). While *The Sisters* and *The Cardinal* belong together, the printing of *The Doubtful Heir* was a distinct operation; it had at least two
compositors, one of whom is clearly distinguishable by his spelling
from the man responsible for the other two plays; it was set from a
different case or cases round which had accumulated a different set of
ornaments.

   Robert K. Turner has investigated Warren's output round about
1647 when he shared in the production of the Beaumont and Fletcher
Folio. Turner reports that Warren's was a business large enough to
undertake major jobs, and that he printed books concurrently.[92] The
evidence about the printing of his share of the six plays, coupled with
a sizeable list of other publications, some of them substantial,[93] suggests that his trade did not contract. If as a result his printing practice
remained the same, there may be an explanation for a bibliographical
oddity found in *The Cardinal*.

   There are two sets of running-titles for *The Cardinal*. These are not transferred consistently to the two formes of the next gathering but change places within the forme and even change formes. The usual advantage of two-skeleton printing was that the compositor could set and impose one forme while the other was on the press, but the press must have been empty of *The Cardinal* while both sets of running-titles were imposed.[94] Despite the two skeletons, printing could proceed no faster than by the one-skeleton method. The only sign of speeding-up comes with gathering F whose running-titles all come from the inner forme of E. Presumably the outer forme of E was still on the press. The abnormal disposition of running-titles at least makes another slight peculiarity understandable. Two skeletons imply two compositors, working at two cases, keeping up with the press-work. There is no evidence whatsoever that *The Cardinal* had more than one compositor. Although the spelling is not wholly regular, variation is infrequent and forms no pattern; and there is either consistency or random deviation in all the incidental details of speech headings, catchwords, comma spacing, and so on. Also since broken type from inner B recurs in both formes of all succeeding sheets, the supposition is that only one case was in use. Since the two skeletons were manifestly not used to speed work along, the single compositor is not an anomaly.

The mixing of running-titles is probably explained by Warren's concurrent printing. Instead of the scenario of smoothly dovetailed composition and press-work leading to the rapid completion of one book we have to imagine a slower progress on single books, with two or more pieces of work under way at the same time. The signs in *The Cardinal* are of some delay, but not major hold-ups. The recurrence of broken type points to a regular setting of inner and then outer formes with only one instance of type in successive formes.[95] Thus each forme must have been composed before its immediate predecessor, but only its immediate predecessor, was distributed. The skeletons with their running-titles must have been on the imposing stone together since every change-over left some running-titles in exactly the same position. Such a procedure means that the press was sometimes free, although the compositor was probably kept busy, given the number of pages in an octavo forme. While he laboured, the same press could be used to print part of another book or some more ephemeral pamphlet. Presumably the delays occurred between completed sheets.

The printing is on the whole careful; apart from a few turned letters and instances of foul case, the worst mistakes are mispunctu-

ation. The text was proof-corrected with a rather cursory conscien-
tiousness. Errors remain—extra letters, wrong punctuation—but
minor details are noticed and corrected, the press in some instances
being stopped twice. Only one change indicates reference to
copy—the addition of 'Hereafter' at IV.ii.270.[96] The proof-
correction does not seem to be authorial, although Shirley *could* have
seen the play through the press. In 1652 he had no theatre to write
for; several of his editors have suggested that he saw various plays
through the press;[97] and he provided a dedication for each of the six
plays. But *The Cardinal*'s press-corrections bear the mark of the
printing-house. Many are obvious corrections of punctuation, some
look like printing-house standardisation, and at least one is wrong;
the addition of a comma after 'cannot' at IV.ii.222 helps to create one
of the few major obscurities in the text. It is unlikely that Shirley
himself was responsible for these changes.

No new edition of *The Cardinal* was published before William
Gifford's 1833 edition of Shirley's complete works. Gifford died
before publication and thus another of the nineteenth century's inde-
fatigable editors, Alexander Dyce, completed the sixth volume and
wrote an introductory essay. Gifford's edition has a nineteenth-
century editor's occasionally cavalier way with the original. Convin-
ced that Octavo betrayed printing-house corruption and defective
syntax, he felt free to emend without bibliographical cause, to excise
colloquial contractions which are now known to be characteristic of
Shirley[98] and to reline in the interests of metrical regularity. Yet all
later editors owe him a great deal; he is responsible for the accepted
scene-divisions and for many necessary stage directions, while more
rigorous editors have accepted some of his relinings.

Gifford was followed, in both senses, by Edmund Gosse, whose
selection of Shirley's plays in the Mermaid Series (1888) owes little
to scholarship. He reproduces Gifford's expansions, punctuation
and line changes, but he does worse. He repeats most of Gifford's
emendations without including warning brackets and silently makes
changes of his own. Five editions were published in the first half of
this century. W. A. Neilson (*The Chief Elizabethan Dramatists*, 1911)
based his text on a Harvard copy of Octavo but was much influenced
by Gifford. H. R. Walley and J. H. Wilson (*Early Seventeenth-
Century Plays*, 1930) claimed to have produced a text based on the
first edition and on Gifford and Gosse; the modern versions seem the
more influential. Two better editions follow, by C. F. T. Brooke and
N. Paradise (*English Drama*, 1933), and by C. R. Baskervill, V. B.

Heltzel and A. H. Nethercot (*Elizabethan and Stuart Plays*, 1934). Brooke and Paradise consulted the first edition and restored some of its readings although they were influenced by Gifford's line-divisions and by some of his readings. Baskervill and his collaborators used Gifford and a Library of Congress copy. They too restore older readings and also some of the original line-divisions. Theirs is the most reliable of the early modern editions. In 1935, E. W. Parks and R. C. Beatty published in *The English Drama* another version heavily dependent on Gifford. Like Gosse they are guilty of concealing emendations. In much of the detail of punctuation Neilson is their model.

There are two more recent editions. The best of all modern editions is Charles Forker's old-spelling text (1965), grounded in modern bibliographical method and with a wide-ranging introduction and thorough annotation. Forker restores most of the original readings and much of the original lineation. His textual account is incomplete—he was able to collate only six copies and thus missed much proof-correction—but given the nature of the proof-correction, the text is little affected by a failure to collate more copies. Inevitably he influenced the remaining editor, Robert G. Lawrence, whose *Jacobean and Caroline Tragedies* (1974) includes *The Cardinal*, oddly described as Shirley's 'only tragedy' (p. 184). Lawrence reproduces some of Forker's stage directions, and like Forker restores some original lineation and the reference to Valeria at I.ii.97. On his own account he cuts a good deal of punctuation. He is also the only editor in a position to incorporate Frank Manley's suggestion that Hernando does not commit suicide but is fatally wounded in a scuffle with the Cardinal's supporters.[99]

Excerpts from *The Cardinal* are in anthologies by W. H. Williams, *Specimens of the Elizabethan Drama* (Oxford, 1905), and Thomas Campbell, *Specimens of the British Poets*, 7 vols. (London, 1819), IV.

The present edition is based on the 1653 Octavo. I have collated 43 copies, 16 from microfilm or xerox, 27 from the originals, and know of three others, whose press-corrections have beecn checked for me. The results are inevitably out of proportion to the labour involved but at least such a large number of surviving copies comes close to guaranteeing complete information. I have examined all modern editions but my collation in the present text is not historical. I include significant substantive variants but have ignored unfounded emendations by earlier editors. I also include those stage directions which derive from earlier editions. All proof-corrections are collated and also listed in Appendix I where I have noted any minor disturbances of type related to proof-correction. Since few of the changes seem authoritative I have assessed each alteration separately and have in some cases retained the uncorrected version. Where Gifford's overenthusiastic relinings are accepted by the more judicious Forker I have collated them.

The spelling, in accordance with Revels principles, is modernised but the punctuation is closer to the original. This practice requires some justification. The surviving Shirley manuscript, *Don Manuell*, is punctuated mainly with commas and semi-colons, and the short sections in Shirley's own hand show the playwright punctuating no more heavily than his scribe. *The Cardinal* also makes liberal use of the comma, with semi-colons for longer pauses, as do several other Shirley first editions.[100] Not only may the punctuation be authorial but it has a faster tempo than does the modern sentence with its reliance on the period. In an attempt to maintain the pace of the original I have reproduced its punctuation wherever I can, but some modernisation has been unavoidable for the sake of clarity. I have of course altered manifest inaccuracies.

I think Octavo contains some mislinings but have been more cautious than Gifford in my corrections.[101] Some of Gifford's relinings merely change the position of the short lines, and several times he depends on inserted words to regularise the metre. And even allowing for a copyist's errors, what I can reconstruct of Shirley's practice suggests that he did not fully regularise conversational passages. I can, for instance, find no way of cobbling II.i.136–56 into pentameters. On three occasions (I.i.61–72, IV.iii.81–4, V.ii.5–11) I have noticed possible alterations but have not been persuaded of their inevitability. I comment on these in the notes.

I follow Gifford's scene-division, and the usual Revels principles as outlined in the General Editors' Introduction. I deviate from the Revels practice in one detail; the Duchess and the Cardinal are the central characters and so I have dignified their titles with capital letters. Abbreviated stage directions and speech headings are silently expanded. Since Shirley is a dramatist of echoes my annotation is generous with parallel passages, especially when these occur in others of the *Six New Playes*.

NOTES

1 For a full account of Shirley's life, see Bas, ch. 1, and *The Lady of Pleasure* in the Revels Series. For Shirley's domestic service, see J. P.

Feil, 'James Shirley's Years of Service', *R.E.S.*, N.S., VIII (1957), 413–16. For his later teaching career see Vivian Salmon, 'James Shirley and some problems of 17th century grammar', *Archiv*, CXCVII (1961), 287–96, and Wood, II, 377.

2 Bas (pp.40–2) rejects Marvin Morillo's argument that in 1632 Shirley was employed in Henrietta Maria's household ('Shirley's "Preferment" and the Court of Charles I', *S.E.L.*, I, Spring, 1961, 101–17).

3 See Allan H. Stevenson, 'Shirley's Years in Ireland', *R.E.S.*, XX (1944), 19–28. It is not certain why Shirley went to Ireland. There was plague in London but Davenant, for instance, remained there. Bas argues (p. 48) that Shirley was unemployed, since the remaining major companies already had dramatists.

4 For information about Shirley's impeachment in January 1650/1, see Armstrong, p.xv. Bas (p. 60) thinks Shirley must have lied about how much he possessed. The will is reproduced by Nason, pp. 158–60, and by Bas, pp.605–6.

5 Wood, II, 378.

6 Shirley may have had a contract with Christopher Beeston (Bentley, V, 1068). Elsewhere Bentley cites from Brome's contract the demand for a regular supply of scripts and argues that Shirley's conditions of work were probably similar (*Profession*, pp. 120–2).

7 Prologue to *The Cardinal*, ll. 15–16.

8 *The Politician* has no performance licence recorded. Its links with *The Gentleman of Venice* indicate a date round about 1639 (Bentley, V, 1138).

9 Gerard Langbaine, *An Account of the English Dramatick Poets* (Oxford, 1691), deems Shirley 'Chief of the Second-rate Poets' (p. 474).

10 February 1640/1 had seen the latest petition against the theatre by the Puritans of Blackfriars and other parishes (Bentley, VI, 39).

11 Herbert, p. 39. The season seems to have run from November till early summer. Shirley's plays were *Rosania* (*The Doubtful Heir*), licensed 1 June 1640; *The Imposture*, 10 November 1640; *The Politic Father* (*The Brothers*), 26 May 1641; *The Cardinal*; *The Sisters*, 26 April 1642. *The Court Secret* was probably intended for November 1642 (Bentley, I, 63).

12 Karl Fröhlich, *Quellenstudien zu einigen Dramen James Shirley's* (Herford, 1913), pp. 72–80. *El buen vecino* was first published in *Parte treinta y tres de doze Comedias famosas de varios autores* (Valencia, 1642). Its authorship is doubtful (*Obras de Lope de Vega*, 13 vols., Madrid, 1916–30, IV, v), and its publication date means that any knowledge Shirley had of the play came from some other source.

13 *Obras de Lope de Vega*, IV, 1–29.

14 'Fear neither the king nor the world.'

15 Bowers, p. 229.

16 There are other minor verbal similarities, and both villains admit they have trapped themselves (*Sicily and Naples*, p. 73—misnumbered 93; *The Cardinal*, V.iii.273).

17 They also share the name Antonio, the phrase '*Cum privilegio*' (*The Rebellion*, sig. H1v; *The Cardinal*, V.ii.38), and the structure of 'you a Player, you a Plasterer' (*The Rebellion*, sig. I1v; *The Cardinal*, III.ii.64–5).

18 Gifford, Gosse, Neilson, Brooke, Parks, Forker, and Lawrence mention

Webster. For detail, see Forker, pp. xlviii–liii and Fröhlich, pp. 78–80. See also Kathleen McLuskie, 'The plays and the playwrights: 1613–1642', *The Revels History of Drama in English*, vol. IV, ed. Lois Potter (London and New York, 1981), 250.

19 Bowers (p. 229) finds a closer resemblance to Hernando in Hamond in Beaumont and Fletcher's *The Bloody Brother*; in revenging his own injury he takes over Edith's task of vengeance. Echoes from *White Devil* as well as *Duchess of Malfi* suggest a general Websterian influence rather than the specific relationship of two plays (see Forker, pp. lii–liii).

20 See Bowers, p. 228, for a more detailed comparison.

21 See Forsythe and the notes to the present edition. The other five of Shirley's *Six New Playes* are full of anticipations and memories of *The Cardinal*.

22 Boas, p. 376; Forker, pp. xxxvii–xlvii. Forker notes the possible influence of *H8*, II.iv and III.i, where Wolsey confronts Katherine.

23 *C.S.P.D.*, 1635, pp. viii–ix. In the years preceding the writing of *The Cardinal* many cases are recorded of men arraigned for accusing Laud of popery, e.g. *C.S.P.D.*, 1633–4, p. 207; 1634–5, p. 22; 1638–9, pp. 213–14. For a general study of Caroline drama's interest in politics see Frank Occhiogrosso, 'Sovereign and Subject in Caroline Tragedy' (unpublished doctoral dissertation, Johns Hopkins University, 1969).

24 See Forsythe, pp. 96–7. Official reaction against *The Cardinal's Conspiracy* in 1639 (Bentley, *Profession*, pp. 180–1) indicates why Shirley could not earlier have risked this particular villain.

25 See pp. 19–20.

26 *Shakespeare's Tragedies and Other Studies in Seventeenth Century Drama* (London, 1950), pp. 161 and 178.

27 '"Wits most accomplished Senate"'; The Audience of the Caroline Private Theaters', *S.E.L.*, XVIII (1978), 341–60.

28 G. E. Bentley, 'The Diary of a Caroline Theatergoer', *M.P.*, XXXV (1937–8), 61–72 (p. 72); Arthur C. Kirsch, 'A Caroline Commentary on the drama', *M.P.*, LXVI (1968–9), 256–61.

29 Leech, p. 178; Neill, p. 356.

30 See pp. 11–12.

31 For Shirley's comments on his plots, see prologues to *The Brothers* and *The Doubtful Heir* (I, 191; IV, 279).

32 Alfred Harbage, *Cavalier Drama*, (New York 1936), p. 165; Jakob Schipper, *James Shirley. Sein Leben und Seine Werke* (Vienna and Leipzig, 1911), p. 355. See also Bas, pp. 187–9, and Forker, pp. lxii–lxv.

33 *The Complete Works of Algernon Charles Swinburne*, ed. Edmund Gosse and Thomas Wise, 20 vols. (London, 1925–7), XII, 340. In 1885, Swinburne discouraged A. C. Bullen from editing Shirley's plays (*The Swinburne Letters*, ed. Cecil Y. Lang, 6 vols., New Haven, 1959–62, V, 95, 96, and 118).

34 See also *Love's Cruelty*, ed. John F. Nims, Garland Renaissance Drama (New York and London, 1980), p. lxi.

35 *Complete Works*, XII, 363.

36 Emrys Jones (*Scenic Form in Shakespeare*, Oxford, 1971, p. 69) cites the argument that this kind of twofold structure was common in Elizabethan drama.

37 See Forsythe, p. 71.

38 Flaviano pretends conversion in *The Imposture*, II.i (Forsythe, p. 71), but in the earlier play the audience is alerted to falsehood. Cf. Dekker's *Match Me in London*, III.i (Forker): Don John eats grapes with Valasco, pretends to be poisoned and sends for an antidote. Valasco drinks and falls—but Don John has himself been deceived with a sleeping potion instead of poison.

39 A 'disingenuous' stratagem, review of Gifford, *The American Quarterly Review*, XVI (1834), 103–66, p. 163; see also Boas, p. 375.

40 Boas, p. 377; also Bas, p. 252.

41 Shirley liked to save the truly innocent—Albina in *The Politician*, Eubella in *Love's Cruelty*.

42 Harvey, *Ciceronianus*, introd. H. S. Wilson, trans. C. A. Forbes, Studies in the Humanities, 4 (Lincoln, Nebraska, 1945), p. 63. Jonson (*Wks.*, VIII, 622) echoes John Hoskins's *Directions for Speech and Style* (1590), ed. H. H. Hudson (Princeton, 1935), p. xxvii.

43 See the verses by Edmund Colles, John Fox, Philip Massinger, and John Jackson (Gifford, I, lxix, lxxiii, lxxix, and lxxxviii–lxxxix). *The Cardinal* does however have some murky patches (Gifford, V, 300n.).

44 But see Felix E. Schelling, *Elizabethan Drama 1558–1642*, 2 vols. (Boston and New York, 1908), II, 326 ('limpid and perspicuous'); W. H. Williams, *Specimens of the Elizabethan Drama* (Oxford, 1905), p. 418 ('graceful, fluent, and perspicuous').

45 'James Shirley's Uses of *Language*', *S.E.L.*, VI (1966), 323–39 (pp. 332 and 339). Cf. Nason's praise of *The Cardinal*'s intellectual unity (p. 346).

46 'Of Complements', *Essayes* (1600–1), ed. Don Cameron Allen (Baltimore, Md., 1946), pp. 90–1.

47 *The Letters of Dorothy Osborne to William Temple*, ed. G. C. Moore Smith (Oxford, 1928), p. 91 (September 1653).

48 *The Fortescue Papers*, ed. Samuel R. Gardiner, Camden Society (London, 1871), p. 128 (May 1620); *Letters and Papers of the Verney Family*, ed. John Bruce, Camden Society (London, 1853), p. 125 (July 1626); *The Oxinden Letters, 1607–1642*, ed. Dorothy Gardiner (London, 1933), p. 105 (July 1635); *The Autobiography and Correspondence of Sir Simonds D'Ewes*, ed. James O. Halliwell, 2 vols. (London, 1845), II, 294 (July 1642).

49 Philomusus (John Gough), augmented 7th ed. (1646).

50 Ralph Verney's tutor wrote to his protégé in 1633: 'what else the court may alter in others, it hath not made you soe little reall as to measure a friend by a compliment', *Memoirs of the Verney Family During the Civil War*, ed. Frances P. Verney, 2 vols. (London, 1892), I, 124–5.

51 Shirley may himself have perpetrated a compliment book. *Wits Labyrinth* by 'J. S.' (1648) was tentatively attributed by Malone (in his copy, now in the Bodleian Library) to Shirley.

52 One counter to the formality is Shirley's characteristic colloquial contraction (wo', sho', 'em). See Cyrus Hoy, 'The Shares of Fletcher and his Collaborators in the Beaumont and Fletcher Canon (IV)', *S.B.*, XII (1959), 91–116 (p. 109); Ronald M. Huebert, 'On Detecting John Ford's Hand: A Fallacy', *The Library*, XXVI (1971), 256–9.

53 Forker, p. lxix, and George Saintsbury (*A History of English Prosody*, 3

vols., London, 1906–10, II, 308) praise Hernando's speech.

54 Clifford Leech, *The John Fletcher Plays* (London, 1962), p. 137.
55 Eugene M. Waith, *The Pattern of Tragicomedy in Beaumont and Fletcher* (New Haven, 1952), pp. 24–5.
56 *Themes and Conventions of Elizabethan Tragedy* (Cambridge, 1935), p. 266; see also Baskervill, p. 1577.
57 *Shakespeare's Tragedies and Other Studies in Seventeenth Century Drama*, p. 40.
58 Nason, writing of Shirley's London comedies, p. 287; see also S. J. Radtke, *James Shirley: His Catholic Philosophy of Life* (Washington, D.C., 1929).
59 'Tragedy, Justice and the Subject', *1642: Literature and Power in the Seventeenth Century*, ed. Francis Barker and others (Colchester, 1981), pp. 166–86.
60 See pp. 5–6 for some contemporary historical parallels.
61 See the account of *The Red Snake* on pp. 29–30.
62 *James Shirley, Dramatiker der Decadenz*, Swiss Studies in English, xxx (Berne, 1952), p. 58.
63 *The Family, Sex and Marriage in England, 1500–1800* (London, 1977), p. 307.
64 For instance in *Honoria and Mammon*.
65 But Columbo's revenge offends court etiquette (Richard Morton, 'Deception and Social Dislocation: An Aspect of James Shirley's Drama', *Renaissance Drama*, IX, 1966, 227–45, p. 233).
66 Howard, preface to *The Womens Conquest*, sig. A3v; Dibdin, *A Complete History of the English Stage*, 5 vols. (London, 1797–1800), IV, 45; Thomas M. Parrott and Robert H. Ball, *A Short View of Elizabethan Drama* (New York, 1943), p. 277; Nason, p. 361; Bowers, p. 230; Schelling, *Elizabethan Drama*, II, 428.
67 Bas, p. 341, thinks Shirley was too fundamentally optimistic and orthodox about man and his destiny to write tragedy.
68 Richard Hosley, 'A Reconstruction of the Second Blackfriars', *The Elizabethan Theatre I*, ed. David Galloway (Toronto, 1969), pp. 74–88, thinks the stage was relatively small. See the counter-argument in David Whitmarsh-Knight, 'The Second Blackfriars: The Globe Indoors', *T.N.*, XXVII (1972–3), 94–8.
69 See T. J. King, *Shakespearean Staging, 1599–1642* (Cambridge, Mass., 1971). King queries the methods and findings of Irwin Smith, *Shakespeare's Blackfriars Playhouse* (London, 1966).
70 'Perspective Scenery and the Caroline Playhouses', *T.N.*, XXVII (1972–3), 98–113.
71 The prologue is assigned to *The Cardinal* in Shirley's *Poems, etc.* (1646) but attached to *The Sisters* in *Six New Playes*. See Appendix II.
72 Herbert, p. 118. The details of the actors who may have played in this production are taken from E. Nungezer, *A Dictionary of Actors* (New Haven, 1929), and John Downes, *Roscius Anglicanus*, ed. Montague Summers (London, n.d.). The Leeds copy also names, in a different hand, eight Caroline actors, but since three of those named (John Rice, Nicholas Tooley and John Honyman) had either left the company or were dead by 1636 the list must simply be an uninformed guess. The

other actors listed are Robert Benfield, Thomas Pollard, John Lowin, Joseph Taylor, and Richard Robinson. Oct. records that Thomas Pollard spoke the epilogue.

73 *The Diary of Samuel Pepys*, ed. R. C. Latham and W. Matthews (London, 1970–83), III, 211–12; VIII, 399; IX, 177.

74 Genest, *The English Stage, 1660–1830*, 10 vols. (Bath, 1832), VII, 238–40.

75 London, 1796.

76 Eric Shorter, *Daily Telegraph*, February 1970; *Farnham Herald*, February 1970.

77 *Daily Telegraph, Surrey and Hants. Newsletter, Farnham Herald*, all February 1970.

78 Doug Shaffer, *San Francisco Bay Guardian*, 1 February 1979.

79 Valeria becomes Val, Celinda Seely, and Hernando Hern.

80 *San Francisco Bay Guardian*, 1 February 1979.

81 *San Francisco Chronicle*, 15 January 1979.

82 *San Francisco Chronicle*, 8 January 1979.

83 For instance, the British Museum's 1346.b.34. Surviving copies are listed in Appendix I.

84 F's running-titles are all from inner E—see Fredson Bowers, 'Running-title Evidence for Determining Half-Sheet Imposition', *S.B.*, I (1948–9), 199–202. In the copies where I have examined the watermark it appears in either A or F, a pattern consistent with half-sheet imposition (J. R. Mulryne, 'The Imposition of Initial and Final Half-Sheets in an Octavo', and 'Half-Sheet Imposition and Running-Title Transfer in *Two New Plays by Thomas Middleton*, 1657', *The Library*, 5th Series, XXX, 1975, 229–32 and 222–8).

85 See note on III.ii.0.1. At one point in Oct., *Fifth Servant* becomes *another* (III.ii.56.1) although the dialogue indicates his identity.

86 See also II.i.53 and 58.

87 The MS in Worcester College Library entitled *Don Manuell* is an early draft of *The Court Secret*. See R. G. Howarth, *R.E.S.*, VII (1931), 302–13, and *R,E.S.*, VIII (1932), 203.

88 'Shirley's Revisions and the Date of *The Constant Maid*', *R.E.S.*, N.S., XVII (1966), 141–8 (p. 147). Howarth says there is no evidence that Shirley made or allowed transcripts of his MS plays (*R.E.S.*, VII, 1931, 302)—an odd statement since Howarth himself describes a transcript. Shirley transcripts are suggested by Sister Martin Flavin, *The Wedding*, Garland Renaissance Drama (New York and London, 1980), p. 9, and Dana McKinnon, *The Ball*, unpublished doctoral dissertation, University of Illinois, 1965.

89 C. William Miller, 'A London Ornament Stock: 1598–1683', *S.B.* VII (1955), 125–51. Miller notes that Wilson signed less than 50 per cent of his output. Wing records Warren as signing few of his books in full, but the ornaments in books signed T. W. indicate that the bulk of these are his.

90 W. W. Greg, *A Bibliography of the English Printed Drama to the Restoration*, 4 vols. (London, 1939–59), III, 1124; Forker, p. xxiii.

91 There are clear examples of sig. A2's M in Nathaniel Hardy, *Thankfulness in Grain*, printed by T. W. (1652), p. 1, and of sig. B1's T in John Chetwind, *The Dead Speaking*, printed by T. W. (1653), sig. A2.

92 'The Printers and the Beaumont and Fletcher Folio of 1647: Section 1 (Thomas Warren's)', *S.B.*, XXVII (1974), 137–56 (p. 138).

93 Listed in Wing index under T. W.

94 The practice is recorded elsewhere: Thomas L. Berger, 'The Printing of *Henry V*, Q1', *The Library*, 6th Series, 1 (1979), 114–25; Fredson Bowers, 'The Printing of *Hamlet*, Q2', *S.B.*, VII (1955), 41–50; J. R. Mulryne, *The Library*, 5th Series, XXX (1975), 222–8.

95 An *A* which appears on outer B (B1) closely resembles in some copies an *A* on inner C (C8), which was set and printed next, as was the normal practice. Normally in *The Cardinal* type from the second forme of a sheet reappears only in the second forme of the next sheet, the usual pattern when setting by formes (Robert K. Turner, Jr., 'The Printing of *A King and No King* Q1', *S.B.*, XVIII, 1965, 255–61). If this is the same *A*, outer B must have been partially distributed (perhaps because *A* was in short supply) before composition of inner C was complete.

96 In uncorrected copies, something is obviously missing; the corrector would be compelled to consult the MS to fill in the gap. For details of other corrections see Appendix I. The lack of proof-correction in E may be another sign of faster progress at this stage.

97 *The Bird in a Cage*, ed. Frances Senescu (New York and London, 1980), p. xix; *The Wedding*, ed. Sister Martin Flavin, p. 8; *The Politician*, ed. Robert J. Fehrenbach (New York and London, 1980), p. lix; *St Patrick for Ireland*, ed. John P. Turner (New York and London, 1979), p. 20 (all Garland Renaissance Drama). See also Bentley, V, 1094, on *Love in a Maze*.

98 See note 52.

99 V.iii.181.1. See 'The Death of Hernando in Shirley's "Cardinal"', *N.Q.*, N.S., XII (1965), 342–3.

100 See *The Bird in a Cage*, ed. Senescu, p. xiii, and *St Patrick for Ireland*, ed. Turner, p. 12; also *The Humorous Courtier*, ed. Marvin Morillo (New York and London, 1979), p. 89; *Love's Cruelty*, ed. John F. Nims (New York and London, 1980), p. xxxiv (both Garland Renaissance Drama).

101 My relinings: I.i.64–5; I.ii.85–6, 92–3; II.i.87, 134–5, 155–6; V.ii.20–2; V.iii.98–9 (following Neilson), 172–3, 241–2, 271–2. Relinings shared with Gifford: I.i.36–7, 48–9, 50–1; II.i.6–7, 49–50, 94–5; II.ii.52–3; II.iii.50–1, 60–3, 121–7; III.i.42, 51–2; III.ii.148–9; IV.ii.16–17, 83–4; IV.iii.26–7; V.ii.102–3; V.iii.93–4, 127–8. Gifford's relinings: I.i.17–22, 43–4, 62–4; I.ii.85–6; II.i.60–1, 83, 86, 132, 134–6, 155–7; II.ii.44; II.iii.79–80; III.i.17–18, 48, 74–5; III.ii.216, 217–219; IVi.15–16, 47–8; IV.ii.5, 198–9, 270; V.ii.30–1, 34, 116; V.iii.186, 216, 218.

THE CARDINAL

A Tragedy

[DEDICATION]

To my worthily honoured friend G.B., Esq.

Sir,

I did suffer at the first some contention within me and, looking upon myself, was inclined to stifle my ambitious thoughts
in this dedication; but when some time and a happy conversa-   5
tion had preferred me to more acquaintance with you, which
was more argument to me than the fame I had heard of your
reputation with the most temperate and ingenious men, I
found you not only an excellent judge, but a good man: at this
my modesty took full encouragement to make this offering,   10
which as I conceive to be the best of my flock, I knew not
a better altar whereon to make it a sacrifice, with this protestation, that it comes—and that is it only which makes all
devotions acceptable—from the heart; and your candid ac-
ceptance will bind me, with all my services and remembrance,   15
to merit a reception with you, in the quality and honour of,
    Sir,
        Your most humble devoted servant,
          JA. SHIRLEY.

[Dedication]. *In italics throughout, Oct.*

1. *G.B.*] probably George Buc, who wrote complimentary verses for
Shirley's *Poems, etc.* (1646) and for the Beaumont and Fletcher Folio (1647).
Buc was related to Sir George Buc, Master of the Revels, who died in 1623.
Although described here as a good man, Buc was a dishonest writer who
published Sir George's work as his own (Mark Eccles, 'The Young Preten-
der', *Thomas Lodge and Other Elizabethans*, ed. C. J. Sisson, 1933, repr.
London, 1966, pp. 485–503).

5. *conversation*] familiarity.

6. *preferred*] a favourite word with Shirley (Bas, p. 376).

8. *temperate*] dispassionate.

ingenious] discerning; another favourite (Bas, p. 376).

11. *best . . . flock*] See Prologue, l. 24, and Epilogue, l. 7.

14. *from the heart*] with the sincerest feeling; stock polite phrase, first
recorded in 1594 (*O.E.D.*, Heart, sb., 34).

44

[COMMENDATORY VERSES]

To the surviving honour and ornament of the English scene,
James Shirley.

As fate, which doth all human matters sway,
Makes proudest things grow up into decay,
And when they are to envied greatness grown,
She wantonly falls off and throws them down:
So, when our English drama was at height,   5
And shined, and ruled with majesty and might,
A sudden whirlwind threw it from its seat,
Deflowered the groves, and quenched the Muses' heat.
Yet as in saints and martyred bodies, when
They cannot call their blessed souls again   10
To earth, relics and ashes men preserve,
And think they do but what, blest, they deserve:
So I, by my devotion led, aspire
To keep alive your noble vestal fire,
Honour this piece, which shows, sir, you have been   15
The last supporter of the dying scene;
And though I do not tell you how you dress
Virtue in glories, and bold vice depress;
Nor celebrate your lovely Duchess' fall,
Or the just ruin of your Cardinal;   20
Yet this I dare assert, when men have named

---

11. earth, relics and] *Subst. Gifford;* earth; Reliques, and *Oct.*   12. do but
what, blest,] *Forker;* do, but what, blest *Oct.*

---

7. *sudden whirlwind*] the Puritan rebellion, which closed the theatres in
1642. Shirley also uses the whirlwind image (see IV.ii.287n.).

8. *Muses'*] Melpomene, Muse of tragedy, and Thalia, Muse of comedy.

13–15. *aspire . . . Honour*] either 'aspire . . . and honour' or 'aspire to keep
alive . . . and to honour'.

14. *vestal fire*] the fire tended by virgins in the temple of the Roman goddess
Vesta.

16. *scene*] stage, standing for 'dramatic art'; antedates *O.E.D.*, 2 (1682).

18. *depress*] discredit.

45

Jonson, the nation's laureate, the famed
Beaumont, and Fletcher, he that wo' not see
Shirley the fourth, must forfeit his best eye.

HALL.   25

22–4. *Jonson . . . Shirley*] Hall ignores Shakespeare; Shirley in the prologue to *The Sisters,* mentions Shakespeare, Fletcher and Jonson (see Appendix II).

25.HALL] possibly one of two John Halls (Gifford, I, xc–xci). The first wrote commendatory verses for *The Grateful Servant* (1630). More likely is another John Hall, of Durham (1627–56), who with Shirley belonged to a group apparently patronised by Thomas Stanley (G. E. Bentley, *H.L.Q.,* II, 1938–9, 219–31). They all contributed poems in praise of Stanley's *Poems and Translations* (1647): Hall's verses, like the lines here, mention the vestal virgins. Shirley and Stanley both wrote commendatory verses for Hall's *Horae Vacivae* (1646). Bas doubts this Hall's authorship since he transferred his support to Parliament about 1648. Yet the parliamentarian Thomas May remained Shirley's friend, and although the references in l. 9 may suggest one Roman Catholic addressing another (Bas, p. 787, n. 71) they are also appropriate from an old friend to his Catholic friend (if Shirley *was* a Roman Catholic). But the surname is common; Harding's *Sicily and Naples* has dedicatory verses by Edward, John and S. Hall. Normally the attribution included the Christian name or initials. The omission of a Christian name and of a catchword in Oct. perhaps indicates disturbance in the printing-house.

PERSONS

KING OF NAVARRE.

CARDINAL.

COLUMBO, the Cardinal's nephew.

[COUNT D']ALVAREZ.

HERNANDO, a colonel.

ALPHONSO[, a captain].

[2] Lords.

[ANTONIO,] *Secretary to the Duchess.*

[2] Colonels.

[2 Captains and other Officers.]

[Soldier.]

ANTONELLI, the Cardinal's servant.

[Gentleman-Usher.]

Surgeon.

Guard.

[Servants, including PEDRO, JAQUES, ROGERO.]

Attendants [, Masquers, Courtiers, Singers].

DUCHESS ROSAURA.

VALERIA, ⎫
CELINDA, ⎭ ladies.

PLACENTIA, a lady that waits upon the Duchess.

SCENE: Navarre.

ALVAREZ] An Alvarez is mentioned in *The Royal Master* (V.i; IV, 178).

ALPHONSO] also a character in *The Young Admiral*.

ANTONIO] in *Duchess of Malfi* but the name is common, especially in *Six New Playes* (in *The Imposture*, *The Sisters* and *The Court Secret*). In s.d. and s.h. Antonio's function as secretary is emphasised.

ANTONELLI] from *White Devil*. See Introduction, n. 19.

PEDRO, JAQUES, ROGERO] all used by Kyd, the first two in *Spanish Tragedy*, the third in *1 Jeronymo*.

ROSAURA] Cf. Rosinda in *The Young Admiral*, Rosania in *The Doubtful Heir*.

PLACENTIA] from present participle of Latin *placere*, 'to please'. Cf. Mrs Placentia in Jonson's *Magnetic Lady* (published 1640, a King's Men's play). In *The Imposture*, Princess Fioretta is left at a place called Placentia (I.i; V, 187).

Prologue

The Cardinal! 'Cause we express no scene,
We do believe most of you gentlemen
Are at this hour in France, and busy there,
Though you vouchsafe to lend your bodies here;
But keep your fancy active till you know,   5
By th' progress of our play, 'tis nothing so;
A poet's art is to lead on your thought
Through subtle paths and workings of a plot,
And where your expectation does not thrive,
If things fall better, yet you may forgive;   10
I will say nothing positive, you may
Think what you please, we call it but a play;
Whether the comic Muse, or lady's love,
Romance, or direful tragedy it prove,
The bill determines not; and would you be   15
Persuaded, I would have't a comedy,

Prologue]. *In italics throughout and placed after the dedication, Oct.*   2. you
gentlemen] *Oct.;* you, gentlemen, *Gifford.*   13. lady's] *This ed.; Ladies
Oct.;* ladies' *Gifford.*

---

1. The Cardinal!] For Shirley's practice of quoting his play-titles, see
Forsythe, p. 93.
'*Cause . . . scene*] because we don't indicate the setting. The published text
specifies Navarre (see foot of p. 84).
3. *Are . . . France*] Cardinal Richelieu would be in the minds of most
Englishmen; still at the height of power in 1641, he died the following year.
See Introduction, p. 6.
4. *vouchsafe*] deign; another fashionable word.
5. *fancy*] imagination.
7–8.] For Shirley's interest in plot, see Introduction, p. 8. Cf. Jonson's
'Words, above action: matter, above words' (*Cynthia's Revels,* Prologue;
Wks., IV, 43).
9–10.] If the play is not as you anticipated, you may forgive it if it turns out
better than you expected.
13. *lady's*] Most edd. print 'ladies'' but 'lady's' seems more appropriate
since it can refer generally to plays about love or more specifically to this play
with its single heroine.
15. *bill*] play-bill; ll. 13–15 indicate that play-bills did not always specify
genre. No play-bills survive from this period (Bentley, *Profession,* p. 61).

For all the purple in the name and state
Of him that owns it; but 'tis left to fate;
Yet I will tell you ere you see it played,
What the author—and he blushed too, when he said   20
(Comparing with his own, for't had been pride,
He thought, to build his wit a pyramid
Upon another's wounded fame), this play
Might rival with his best, and dared to say—
Troth I am out; he said no more; you then,   25
When 't's done, may say your pleasures, gentlemen.

---

17. name and] *Neilson; name, and Oct.*   21. (Comparing . . . own, for't] *This ed.; (Comparing . . . own for't Oct.;* Comparing . . . own, (for't *Gifford;* Comparing . . . own—for't *Walley.*

---

17. *For*] despite.

purple] the crimson colour of the Cardinal's robes and, metaphorically, the high rank associated with the colour. Classical theory found the mingling of royal and common people in comedy indecorous (Parks).

18. *him . . . it*] the Cardinal of the title.

21-4.] Most edd. follow Gifford but there is tautology if 'Comparing with his own' and 'rival with his best' are part of the same grammatical unit. 'Comparing with his own' is more aptly set against 'another's wounded fame'.

21. *Comparing . . . own*] i.e. with his own other plays.

22. *pyramid*] Cf. *The Humorous Courtier*, III.i; IV, 564.

25. *out*] at a loss, nonplussed.

Act I

ACT I, Scene i

Enter two Lords *at one door*, ANTONIO *at the other*.

1 Lord. Who is that?
2 Lord.　　　　　　The Duchess' Secretary.
1 Lord. Signor.
Antonio. Your lordships' servant.
1 Lord. How does her grace since she left her mourning
　　For the young Duke Mendoza, whose timeless death　　5
　　At sea left her a virgin and a widow?
2 Lord. She's now inclining to a second bride;
　　When is the day of mighty marriage
　　To our great Cardinal's nephew, Don Columbo?
Antonio. When they agree; they wo' not steal to church,　　10
　　I guess the ceremonies will be loud and public.
　　Your lordships will excuse me.　　　　　　*Exit.*
1 Lord. When they agree! Alas poor lady, she
　　Dotes not upon Columbo, when she thinks

0.1. ANTONIO] *Gifford; Secretary Oct. (throughout scene).*　3. lordships']
This ed.; Lordships *Oct.;* lordship's *Gifford.*　13. agree!] *Gifford;* agree?
Oct.

---

　3. *lordships'*] Most edd. make Antonio address 1 Lord, who has just spoken
to him. It seems more polite for him to address both, since they are standing
together.
　5. *Mendoza*] common Spanish name. See Marston's *Malcontent*, and
Shirley's *The Court Secret.*
　　timeless] untimely, premature.
　6. *virgin . . . widow*] She was betrothed but not yet married; or perhaps the
marriage was not consummated. See II.i.147–50n.
　7. *inclining*] disposed to accept.
　　bride] bridegroom; a late example of this meaning. Brooke reads 'disposed
to become' a bride again.
　8. *mighty*] socially and politically important.
　10 and 13. *When . . . agree*] (i) when they have chosen a day; (ii) when they
are in accord.

50

Of the young Count D'Alvarez, divorced from her   15
By the king's power.

2 Lord. And counsel of the Cardinal, to advance
His nephew to the Duchess' bed; 'tis not well.

1 Lord. Take heed, the Cardinal holds intelligence
With every bird i'th' air.

2 Lord.   Death on his purple pride,   20
He governs all, and yet, Columbo is
A gallant gentleman.

1 Lord. The darling of the war, whom victory
Hath often courted; a man of daring
And most exalted spirit; pride in him   25
Dwells like an ornament, where so much honour
Secures his praise.

2 Lord.   This is no argument
He should usurp and wear Alvarez' title
To the fair Duchess; men of coarser blood
Would not so tamely give this treasure up.   30

1 Lord. Although Columbo's name is great in war,
Whose glorious art and practice is above
The greatness of Alvarez, yet he cannot
Want soul, in whom alone survives the virtue
Of many noble ancestors, being the last   35
Of his great family.

2 Lord.   'Tis not safe, you'll say,
To wrestle with the king.

36–7. 'Tis . . . king] *Gifford; one line in Oct.*

---

16. *king's power*] Both James I and Charles I interfered frequently in marriages (Stone, pp. 607–8).

17. *counsel*] by the counsel. Cf. the wicked counsellor Cassander in *The Coronation*, who plans to marry his son Lisimachus to the queen.

19–20. *holds . . . With*] receives secret reports from.

20. *purple pride*] another reference to the Cardinal's robes and rank.

23. *darling . . . war*] Cf. 'darling both of war and peace', *The Example*, I.i; III, 293.

25–7. *pride . . . praise*] His pride is an adornment because he has earned enough glory to justify it. The contrast is with the Cardinal's pride.

29. *coarser blood*] meaner birth and, by implication, less delicate behaviour.

32. *art and practice*] Forker sets 'art' against 'practice' but 'art' could mean the practical application of any science. In *H5* 'the art and practic part of life' (I.i.51) is distinct from 'theoric'.

33. *he*] Alvarez.

34. *soul*] 'spirit' (Forker).

1 Lord. More danger if the Cardinal be displeased,
      Who sits at helm of state; Count D'Alvarez
      Is wiser to obey the stream than, by   40
      Insisting on his privilege to her love,
      Put both their fates upon a storm.
2 Lord. If wisdom, not inborn fear, make him compose,
      I like it; how does the Duchess bear herself?
1 Lord. She moves by the rapture of another wheel   45
      That must be obeyed; like some sad passenger,
      That looks upon the coast his wishes fly to,
      But is transported by an adverse wind,
      Sometimes a churlish pilot.
2 Lord. She has a sweet and noble nature.
1 Lord.   That   50
      Commends Alvarez, Hymen cannot tie
      A knot of two more equal hearts and blood.

             Enter ALPHONSO.

2 Lord. Alphonso!
Alphonso.   My good lord.
1 Lord.   What great affair

48–9. wind, / Sometimes] *Gifford;* wind, sometimes/ *Oct.*   50–1. That /
Commends] *Gifford;* /That commends *Oct.*

    42.] endanger their future lives.
    43. *compose*] (i) come to a settlement; (ii) settle the mind.
    45. *rapture . . . wheel*] unexplained. 'Rapture' = 'momentum', but what is
'another wheel'? ('superior force . . . the king' (Gifford); 'steering wheel'
(Baskervill); i.e. 'ship's wheel' but this 'does not produce momentum'
(Forker); 'sphere in Ptolemaic astronomy', 'wheel of a vehicle' (Forker, who
is not happy with his explanations)). Cf. Berinthia, *The Maid's Revenge*, I.ii:
'I move, / Not by a motion I can call my own, / But by a higher rapture, in
obedience / To a father' (I, 108). Perhaps the image is of a cog-wheel. Cf.
Massinger, *The Roman Actor*, III.ii.40 – 'the greater wheeles that move the
lesse' (*Plays*, III, 56); Beaumont and Fletcher, *Women Pleased*, II.v – 'My
love the main wheel that set him a going: / His motion but compell'd' (*Wks.*,
VII, 256). Or 'wheel of Fortune', picking up 'fates' (l. 42).
    46. *sad passenger*] Cf. *The Court Secret*, V.i; V, 502; *The Maid's Revenge*,
III.i; I, 133.
    49. *Sometimes*] which is sometimes.
    51. *Hymen*] the god of marriage.

Hath brought you from the confines?

Alphonso.   Such as will

    Be worth your counsels, when the king hath read   55
    My letters from the governor; the Aragonians,
    Violating their confederate oath and league,
    Are now in arms; they have not yet marched towards us,
    But 'tis not safe to expect, if we may timely
    Prevent invasion.

2 Lord.   Dare they be so insolent?   60

1 Lord. This storm I did foresee.

2 Lord. What have they, but the sweetness of the king,
    To make a crime?

1 Lord.   But how appears the Cardinal
    At this news?

Alphonso.   Not pale, although he knows
    They have no cause to think him innocent,   65
    As by whose counsel they were once surprised.

1 Lord. There is more
    Than all our present art can fathom in
    This story, and I fear I may conclude
    This flame has breath at home to cherish it;   70
    There's treason in some hearts, whose faces are
    Smooth to the state.

---

56. Aragonians,] *Arragonians, corr. Oct.; Arragonians/ uncorr. Oct.*   63.
crime?] *Corr. Oct.;* crime. *uncorr. Oct.*   64–5. Not ... knows / They] *This
ed.;* Not ... although / He *Oct.*

---

54. *confines*] frontier.

56. *Aragonians*] Aragon lies to the east of Navarre. The two states were at
war in 1367, but Shirley makes little attempt to suggest a specific episode of
Iberian history.

57. *confederate oath*] oath of unity.

59. *expect*] wait.

timely] in time.

60. *Prevent*] forestall.

61–72.] could be relined: ... but / ... crime? / ... news? / ... cause / ...
counsel / ... all / ... story, / ... breath / ... in / ... state.

62–3. *What ... crime?*] What, apart from the king's mildness, has
prompted this rebellion?

66. *As ... counsel*] since it was by his counsel.

71. *treason*] the first of several references to treason, possibly implying some
sinister plot by the Cardinal. See Introduction, pp. 20–1.

72. *Smooth*] deceptively friendly.

Alphonso. My lords, I take my leave.
2 Lord.   Your friends, good captain.
                                   Exeunt.

ACT I, Scene ii

Enter DUCHESS, VALERIA, CELINDA.

Valeria. Sweet madam, be less thoughtful, this obedience
     To passion will destroy the noblest frame
     Of beauty that this kingdom ever boasted.
Celinda. This sadness might become your other habit
     And ceremonious black for him that died;   5
     The times of sorrow are expired, and all
     The joys that wait upon the court, your birth,
     And a new hymen that is coming towards you,
     Invite a change.
Duchess.   Ladies, I thank you both;
     I pray excuse a little melancholy   10
     That is behind, my year of mourning hath not
     So cleared my account with sorrow, but there may
     Some dark thoughts stay, with sad reflections,
     Upon my heart for him I lost; even this
     New dress and smiling garment, meant to show   15
     A peace concluded 'twixt my grief and me,
     Is but a sad remembrance: but I resolve
     To entertain more pleasing thoughts, and if
     You wish me heartily to smile, you must
     Not mention grief, not in advice to leave it;   20

---

1. *thoughtful*] melancholy.
obedience] yielding.
2. *frame*] human body.
4. *other habit*] the mourning clothes which the Duchess has now discarded.
5. *ceremonious black*] an allusion to mourning as a ritual.
7–8.] the joys that are associated with your being a courtier, well-born and about to marry. Cf. *The Young Admiral*, V.iii: 'All the delights that wait upon a kingdom' (III, 174).
8. *hymen*] wedding. The god's name was often applied to the event.
11. *is behind*] remains.
12. *cleared*] settled.
15. *smiling garment*] bright clothing in contrast to the ceremonious black. See also II.i.120.
18. *entertain*] another favourite word (Bas, p. 376).

Such counsels open but afresh the wounds
Ye would close up; and keep alive the cause,
Whose bleeding you would cure; let's talk of something
That may delight; you two are read in all
The histories of our court; tell me, Valeria,   25
Who has thy vote for the most handsome man?
[*Aside*] Thus I must counterfeit a peace, when all
Within me is at mutiny.

Valeria.   I have examined
All that are candidates for the praise of ladies,
But find—may I speak boldly to your grace?   30
And will you not return it in your mirth,
To make me blush?

Duchess.   No, no; speak freely.

Valeria. I wo' not rack your patience, madam, but
Were I a princess, I should think Count D'Alvarez
Had sweetness to deserve me from the world.   35

Duchess. [*Aside*] Alvarez! She's a spy upon my heart.

Valeria. He's young and active, and composed most sweetly.

Duchess. I have seen a face more tempting.

Valeria.   It had then
Too much of woman in't; his eyes speak movingly,
Which may excuse his voice, and lead away   40
All female pride his captive; his hair black,
Which naturally falling into curls—

Duchess. Prithee no more, thou art in love with him.
The man in your esteem, Celinda, now?

---

27. *Aside*] Subst. Gifford; not in Oct.   36. *Aside*] Subst. Gifford; not in Oct.
She's] shee's *corr. Oct.;* shees *uncorr. Oct.*

25–59. *tell . . . affection*] For similar discussions of suitors, cf. *Mer.V.*, I.ii,
and *Gent.*, I.ii.

31–2. *And . . . blush*] exactly what the Duchess does later. See I.ii.97n.

35.] were charming enough to have first claim on me. Cf. IV.ii.188. Shirley
conflates the idea of Alvarez's worthiness compared to everyone else, with his
choosing a wife from all the women available.

37. *composed . . . sweetly*] charmingly formed.

40. *excuse his voice*] His appearance is so attractive that he does not need to
say anything. See Valeria's complaint that Columbo's 'talk will fright a lady'
(l. 55).

42. *curls*] Cf. *White Devil*, IV.ii.195–6: 'We curl'd-hair'd men / Are still
most kind to women.'

C

Celinda. Alvarez is, I must confess, a gentleman   45
  Of handsome composition, but with
  His mind, the greater excellence, I think
  Another may delight a lady more,
  If man be well considered; that's Columbo,
  Now, madam, voted to be yours.
Duchess.   [*Aside*] My torment!   50
Valeria. [*Aside*] She affects him not.
Celinda. He has person, and a bravery beyond
  All men that I observe.
Valeria.   He is a soldier,
  A rough-hewn man, and may show well at distance;
  His talk will fright a lady; war and grim-   55
  Faced honour are his mistresses; he raves
  To hear a lute; Love meant him not his priest.
  Again your pardon, madam; we may talk,
  But you have art to choose and crown affection.

      [*Celinda and Valeria walk aside.*]

Duchess. What is it to be born above these ladies   60
  And want their freedom? They are not constrained,
  Nor slaved by their own greatness, or the king's;

---

45. is, I] *Gifford;* is, (I *uncorr. Oct.;* is (I *corr. Oct.*   50. *Aside*] *Subst.*
Gifford; not in Oct.   51. *Aside*] *Neilson; not in Oct.*   55. grim-] *Corr. Oct.;*
grim / *uncorr. Oct.*   58. talk,] *Corr. Oct.;* talk / *uncorr. Oct.*   59.1.]
Gifford; not in Oct.

 45–9.] Cf. the contrast of Arcadius and Seleucus in *The Coronation*, III.ii;
III, 493–4.
 46. *composition*] bodily construction; a later use than *O.E.D.* (16a) records.
 47. *His mind*] refers to 'Another' (Columbo) in l. 48.
 50. *voted*] vowed, devoted.
 51. *affects*] likes.
 52. *person*] good appearance.
 53–7. *He . . . priest*] Columbo resembles many of the stock rough soldiers
of the period's drama. Cf. Hotspur in *1H4* (Forker).
 54. *rough-hewn*] lacking in refinement.
 56. *raves*] is maddened.
 57. *lute*] See V.iii.91 s.d. where the Cardinal enlists a lutenist to aid his
seduction.
 60–4. *What . . . love*] The meditation on the trials of high birth is a set
piece. Cf. *The Politician*, V.ii; V, 168.
 61. *want*] lack, but with a hint of 'desire'.
 62. *slaved*] enslaved.

But let their free hearts look abroad, and choose
By their own eyes to love; I must repair
My poor afflicted bosom, and assume   65
The privilege I was born with; which now prompts me
To tell the king he hath no power nor art
To steer a lover's soul.

Enter ANTONIO.

                              What says Count D'Alvarez?
Antonio. Madam, he'll attend you.
Duchess. Wait you as I directed, when he comes   70
    Acquaint me privately.
Antonio.   Madam, I have news,
    'Tis now arrived the court, we shall have wars.
Duchess. I find an army here of killing thoughts.
Antonio. The king has chosen Don Columbo general,
    Who is immediately to take his leave.   75
Duchess. What flood is let into my heart! How far
    Is he to go?
Antonio.   To Aragon.
Duchess.   That's well
    At first; he should not want a pilgrimage
    To the unknown world, if my thoughts might convey
        him.
Antonio. 'Tis not impossible he may go thither.   80
Duchess. How?
Antonio. To the unknown other world; he goes to fight;

68.1 ANTONIO] *Gifford; Secretary Oct. (throughout scene).*   71. news,] *Oct.;*
news; *Gifford.*   72. court, we] *Oct.;* court; we *Gifford;* court: we *Brooke.*

---

64. *to love*] either 'where to love' (taking up 'abroad') or 'whom to love'.

66. *privilege . . . with*] immunity (from coercion) belonging to her rank.

71–2. *Madam . . . wars*] ambiguous punctuation. Shirley's sentences quite
often hinge round a central clause. The *it* of ''Tis' is both the news and its
content, i.e. that 'we shall have wars'. Gifford divides the sentence into three
statements; Brooke subordinates 'we shall have wars' to the previous clause.

72. *arrived*] reached.

73.] Perhaps the Duchess simply reacts to the news of war; perhaps she
means she is already internally at war.

79. *the unknown world*] ambiguous; perhaps America, the new world
(Forker) but with a strong suggestion of the 'other world' as Antonio (l. 82)
understands it. Cf. V.iii.162.

82. *unknown other world*] death. Cf. *The Doubtful Heir*, III.i; IV, 323, *The
Gamester*, V.ii; III, 277.

That's in his way, such stories are in nature.
Duchess. Conceal this news.
Antonio. He wo' not be long absent; the affair   85
　　Will make him swift to kiss your grace's hand.   [*Exit.*]
Duchess. He cannot fly
　　With too much wing to take his leave; [*To Valeria and*
　　　　Celinda] I must
　　Be admitted to your conference; ye have
　　Enlarged my spirits, they shall droop no more.   90
Celinda. We are happy if we may advance one thought
　　To your grace's pleasure.
Valeria.　　　　　　　　　Your eye before
　　Was in eclipse, these smiles become you, madam.
Duchess. [*Aside*] I have not skill to contain myself.

Enter PLACENTIA.

Placentia. The Cardinal's nephew, madam, Don Columbo.   95
Duchess. Already? Attend him.   *Exit* PLACENTIA.
Valeria.　　　　　　　　　Shall we take our leave?
Duchess. He shall not know, Valeria, how you praised him.
Valeria. If he did, madam, I should have the confidence
　　To tell him my free thoughts.

Enter COLUMBO.

85–6. He . . . hand.] *This ed.;* He . . . absent; / The . . . hand. *Oct.*   86. *Exit.*]
Gifford; not in Oct.   88. *To Valeria and Celinda*] *Subst. Baskervill; not in
Oct.*   92–3. To . . . madam] *This ed.;* To . . . pleasure / Your . . . smiles /
Become . . . Madam *Oct.*   94. *Aside*] *Subst. Gifford; not in Oct.*   97.
Valeria] *Oct.;* Celinda *Gifford.*   98. *Valeria.*] *Val. Oct.; Cel. Gifford.*

83.] Death is a possible outcome in such circumstances. In *The Politician*,
Gotharus sends Turgesius to war in the hope that he will go 'to another world'
(I.i; V, 94).
　86. *kiss . . . hand*] a courtly cliché. Antonio may be speaking straight-
forwardly or may intend to mock Columbo the soldier.
　88. *With . . . wing*] too swiftly.
　89. *conference*] conversation.
　90. *Enlarged*] freed.
　92–3. *Your . . . eclipse*] perhaps a reference to tears, perhaps to eyelids cast
down, perhaps meaning 'gloomy'. Cf. *The Imposture*, IV.v; V, 240.
　97. *Valeria*] Most edd. substitute 'Celinda'. I agree with Forker and
Lawrence in retaining 'Valeria' and reading the Duchess's comment as ironic.
This joke is prepared in ll. 31–2. The later confusion (ll. 134–46) shows that
Shirley had not quite sorted out Valeria and Celinda (Introduction, p. 30).

Duchess. My lord, while I'm in study to requite   100
    The favour you ha' done me, you increase
    My debt to such a sum, still by a new honouring
    Your servant, I despair of my own freedom.
Columbo. Madam, he kisseth your white hand, that must
    Not surfeit in this happiness—and ladies,   105
    I take your smiles for my encouragement;
    I have not long to practise these court tactics.
                    [Kisses Valeria and Celinda.]
Celinda. *[Aside]* He has been taught to kiss.
Duchess.   There's something, sir,
    Upon your brow I did not read before.
Columbo. Does the character please you, madam?
Duchess.   More,   110
    Because it speaks you cheerful.
Columbo.   'Tis for such
    Access of honour as must make Columbo
    Worth all your love; the king is pleased to think
    Me fit to lead his army.
Duchess.   How, an army?
Columbo. We must not use the priest till I bring home   115
    Another triumph, that now stays for me
    To reap it in the purple field of glory.

105. happiness—] *Corr. Oct.;* happiness,— *uncorr. Oct.*   107.1.] *Subst.*
Gifford; not in Oct.   108. *Aside*] *Baskervill; not in Oct.*

---

101. *you*] The Duchess addresses Columbo as 'you' but to Alvarez she
combines 'you' with 'thou' which in this context suggests intimacy.

102–3. *still . . . servant*] by constantly honouring me afresh. 'Honouring' is
a verbal noun (Abbott, §§ 93, 373).

103. *despair . . . freedom*] I fear I shall never be out of your debt. The
Duchess privately despairs of being freed from her engagement. Forker notes
the figurative reference to a debtor's prison.

104. *kisseth . . . hand*] The prediction is fulfilled. Note the old-fashioned,
formal *-eth* ending.

that] refers back to 'he'.

107. *practise*] perform, but with a hint of practising in order to gain
proficiency.

110. *character*] (i) writing; (ii) distinctive feature. Columbo picks up 'read'.

111. *speaks*] shows.

115–17.] Cf. *The Doubtful Heir,* I.i, where Leonario expects his marriage to
follow triumph in battle (IV, 290).

116. *stays*] waits.

117. *it*] i.e. the triumph.

purple] bloody.

Duchess. But do you mean to leave me, and expose
  Yourself to the devouring war? No enemy
  Should divide us; the king is not so cruel.   120
Columbo. The king is honourable, and this grace
  More answers my ambition than his gift
  Of thee and all thy beauty, which I can
  Love, as becomes thy soldier, and fight *She weeps.*
  To come again, a conqueror of thee;   125
  Then I must chide this fondness.

Enter ANTONIO.

Antonio. Madam, the king, and my lord Cardinal. [*Exit.*]

Enter KING, CARDINAL, and Lords.

King. Madam, I come to call a servant from you,
  And strengthen his excuse; the public cause
  Will plead for your consent; at his return   130
  Your marriage shall receive triumphant ceremonies;
  Till then you must dispense.
Cardinal.   [*Aside*] She appears sad
  To part with him—[*To Columbo*] I like it fairly,
   nephew.
Celinda. [*To Valeria*] Is not the general a gallant man?
  What lady would deny him a small courtesy? 135
Valeria. Thou hast converted me, and I begin
  To wish it were no sin.
Celinda. Leave that to narrow consciences.
Valeria.   You are pleasant.
Celinda. But he would please one better. Do such men

---

127. *Exit.*] Gifford; not in Oct. 132. *Aside*] Forker; not in Oct. 133. *To Columbo*] Subst. Baskervill; not in Oct. 134–46.] S.h. transposed in Oct. 134. *To Valeria*] Subst. Forker; not in Oct.

---

121. *grace*] privilege (of being general).
124. *soldier*] trisyllabic.
124–5. *fight . . . again*] fight to return to.
126. *fondness*] foolish affection.
128. *servant*] lover, and a reminder that Columbo must obey the king.
134–46. Celinda.] Oct. confuses *Cel.* and *Val.* in its s.h. See I.ii.97n. For a similar contrast of attitudes see the princess's ladies in Beaumont and Fletcher's *Philaster.*
138. *You are pleasant*] You're joking.

Lie with their pages?

Valeria.   Wouldst thou make a shift?   140

Celinda. He is going to a bloody business;
 'Tis pity he should die without some heir;
 That lady were hard-hearted now that would
 Not help posterity, for the mere good
 O'th' king and commonwealth.   145

Valeria. Thou art wild, we may be observed.

Duchess. [*To the King*] Your will must guide me, happiness
  and conquest
 Be ever waiting on his sword.

Columbo.   Farewell.

   Exeunt KING, COLUMBO, CARDINAL, Lords.

Duchess. Pray give leave to examine a few thoughts,
 Expect me in the garden.

Ladies.   We attend.   *Exeunt* Ladies.   150

Duchess. This is above all expectation happy;
 Forgive me, virtue, that I have dissembled,
 And witness with me, I have not a thought
 To tempt or to betray him, but secure
 The promise I first made to love and honour.   155

   Enter ANTONIO

Antonio. The Count D'Alvarez, madam.

---

147. *To the King*] *Forker; not in Oct.*   149. thoughts,] *Uncorr. Oct.;*
thoughts; *corr. Oct.*   155. made to] *Oct.;* made, to *Gifford.*

---

139. *please one*] pun on 'pleasant'.

140. *Lie with*] Beaumont and Fletcher's *The Honest Man's Fortune*, III.i,
speaks of Neapolitans teaching French lords to make pages their bedfellows
(*Wks.*, X, 250).

 make a shift] literally 'change clothes' with a page in order to lie with
Columbo, or figuratively, 'attain an end by contrivance'.

141. *bloody business*] See *Mac.*, II.i.48.

142. *die*] perhaps a sexual pun (Forker).

144. *for . . . good*] solely for the good of.

146. *wild*] reckless, licentious.

149. *give leave*] give me leave.

154. *but secure*] to secure, parallel with 'To tempt' and 'to betray'. 'Secure'
could be an imperative, parallel with 'Forgive' and 'witness' (Forker), but this
reading is less likely.

155. *made to*] Oct.'s punctuation suggests that 'love' and 'honour' are
nouns, Gifford's that they are verbs.

Duchess.   Admit him,
    And let none interrupt us;   [*Exit* ANTONIO.]
                    how shall I
    Behave my looks? The guilt of my neglect,
    Which had no seal from hence, will call up blood
    To write upon my cheeks the shame and story   160
    In some red letter.

                    Enter ALVAREZ.

Alvarez.   Madam, I present
    One that was glad to obey your grace, and come
    To know what your commands are.
Duchess.   Where I once
    Did promise love, a love that had the power
    And office of a priest to chain my heart   165
    To yours, it were injustice to command.
Alvarez. But I can look upon you, madam, as
    Becomes a servant, with as much humility—
    In tenderness of your honour and great fortune—
    Give up, when you call back your bounty, all that   170
    Was mine, as I had pride to think them favours.
Duchess. Hath love taught thee no more assurance in
    Our mutual vows, thou canst suspect it possible

157.1.] *Gifford; not in Oct.*

---

158. *Behave*] regulate. Last recorded as transitive verb (*O.E.D.*, 2) in *Tim.*
(1607).

158–61. *The guilt . . . letter*] My sense of guilt at abandoning Alvarez,
which was a deed my heart did not agree to, will summon the blood to expose
my feelings in a blush.

159. *seal*] ratification.

161. *red letter*] The image combines the practice of branding criminals
('shame') with the printing of saints' days in the church calendar in red
('write'). For the latter image, cf. *The Doubtful Heir*, V.iii; IV, 349, and *The
Duke's Mistress*, IV.i; IV, 240, but the suggestion of publicly exposed guilt
points to the former meaning.

165. *chain my heart*] a favourite metaphor; cf. *The Lady of Pleasure*, IV.iii;
IV, 76, *The Doubtful Heir*, I.i and V.iv; IV, 290 and 353.

169. *In tenderness of*] in consideration for.

171. *them*] i.e. acts of bounty.

172–6. *Hath . . . faith*] Note the change from 'you' to 'thou', 'thee'. The
Duchess's reproach is gentle but unwarranted; *she* has become engaged to
someone else.

173. *vows, thou*] vows, than that thou.

I should revoke a promise made to heaven
And thee so soon? This must arise from some   175
Distrust of thy own faith.
Alvarez.   Your grace's pardon.
To speak with freedom, I am not so old
In cunning to betray, nor young in time
Not to see when and where I am at loss,
And how to bear my fortune and my wounds,   180
Which if I look for health must still bleed inward,
A hard and desperate condition;
I am not ignorant your birth and greatness
Have placed you to grow up with the king's grace
And jealousy, which to remove, his power   185
Hath chosen a fit object for your beauty
To shine upon, Columbo, his great favourite;
I am a man on whom but late the king
Has pleased to cast a beam, which was not meant
To make me proud, but wisely to direct   190
And light me to my safety. O, dear madam!
I will not call more witness of my love—
If you will let me still give it that name—
Than this, that I dare make myself a loser,
And to your will give all my blessings up.   195
Preserve your greatness and forget a trifle,
That shall at best, when you have drawn me up,
But hang about you like a cloud, and dim
The glories you are born to.
Duchess.   Misery
Of birth and state! That I could shift into   200
A meaner blood, or find some art to purge
That part which makes my veins unequal; yet

---

178. *to betray*] as to betray. For omission of 'as' see Abbott, § 281.

179. *Not to see*] as not to see.

185. *jealousy*] solicitude.

194. *dare . . . loser*] Shirley and his fellow dramatists were partial to the character who gives up a loved one for his or her own good (Forsythe, p. 67).

196. *greatness*] eminent rank.

199–200. *Misery . . . state*] See note on ll. 60–4. Cf. *Duchess of Malfi*, I.i.441.

202. *That . . . unequal*] The ingredient in her blood which makes it nobler than Alvarez's blood.

Those nice distinctions have no place in us,
There's but a shadow difference, a title,
Thy stock partakes as much of noble sap   205
As that which feeds the root of kings, and he
That writes a lord hath all the essence of
Nobility.

Alvarez.   'Tis not a name that makes
Our separation: the king's displeasure
Hangs a portent to fright us, and the matter   210
That feeds this exhalation is the Cardinal's
Plot to advance his nephew; then Columbo,
A man made up for some prodigious act,
Is fit to be considered; in all three
There is no character you fix upon   215
But has a form of ruin to us both.

Duchess. Then you do look on these with fear.

Alvarez.   With eyes
That should think tears a duty, to lament
Your least unkind fate; but my youth dares boldly
Meet all the tyranny o'th' stars, whose black   220
Malevolence but shoot my single tragedy;
You are above the value of many worlds

---

217. fear.] *Oct.;* fear? *all other edd.*   221. shoot] *Oct.;* shoots *Gifford.*   222.
worlds /] *Corr. Oct.;* worlds, / *uncorr. Oct.*

---

203. *Those nice distinctions*] i.e. of rank.
nice] (i) precise; (ii) senseless.
204. *shadow*] shadow's.
205–6. *Thy . . . kings*] implies that she is of royal blood, Alvarez not.
207. *writes*] describes himself as. 'Signs' is a possible meaning but is not
recorded before 1821.
208–16. *'Tis . . . both*] It's not a mere name that keeps us apart: . . . in any
of the three, whatever distinctive mark (*O.E.D.*, Character, 1) you choose, it
portends our ruin. Or 'character' = 'face' (*O.E.D.*, 10).
210. *a portent*] as a portent.
211. *exhalation*] meteor.
213. *prodigious*] ominous, marvellous; a favourite word (R. G. Howarth,
R.E.S. vii (1931), p. 307, n.1).
214. *Is fit*] needs.
all three] i.e. king, Cardinal, Columbo.
217. *fear*] I retain Oct.'s punctuation since the Duchess may well be making
a statement called forth by Alvarez's words.
221. *shoot*] Gifford's emendation is uncalled-for. Shirley probably wrote
'shoot' with the stars still in his mind.

      Peopled with such as I am.
Duchess.   What if Columbo,
      Engaged to war, in his hot thirst of honour,
      Find out the way to death?
Alvarez.   'Tis possible.   225
Duchess. Or say, no matter by what art or motive,
      He gives his title up, and leave me to
      My own election?
Alvarez.   If I then be happy
      To have a name within your thought, there can
      Be nothing left to crown me with new blessing;   230
      But I dream thus of heaven, and wake to find
      My amorous soul a mockery; when the priest
      Shall tie you to another, and the joys
      Of marriage leave no thought at leisure to
      Look back upon Alvarez, that must wither   235
      For loss of you, yet then I cannot lose
      So much of what I was, once in your favour,
      But in a sigh pray still you may live happy.   *Exit.*
Duchess. My heart is in a mist, some good star smile
      Upon my resolution, and direct   240
      Two lovers in their chaste embrace to meet;
      Columbo's bed contains my winding-sheet.   *Exit.*

---

226. *by . . . motive*] by what trick or for whatever reason.

227. *gives . . . leave*] For the mixing of indicative and subjunctive verbs see Abbott, § 363.

   title] i.e. his claim on the Duchess.

228. *election*] choice.

   be happy] be lucky enough.

232. *My . . . mockery*] My loving heart is deceiving itself (or being deceived).

239. *My . . . mist*] an echo of Webster (*White Devil*, V.vi.260; *Duchess of Malfi*, V.v.94) which is not peculiar to *The Cardinal* but occurs in almost half of Shirley's plays. See also V.iii.282. The image suggests both confusion and tears.

   good star] Cf. ll. 220–1.

242. *winding-sheet*] a favourite image; cf. *The Brothers*, IV.v; I, 252; also common in earlier plays, notably in *White Devil*, II.i.65–6 and 205, and V.vi.157. See also *3H6*, II.v.114.

Act II

Enter General COLUMBO, HERNANDO, *two* Colonels,
ALPHONSO, *two* Captains, *and other* Officers, *as at a council
of war*.

Columbo. I see no face in all this council that
    Hath one pale fear upon't, though we arrived not
    So timely to secure the town, which gives
    Our enemy such triumph.
1 Colonel.   'Twas betrayed.
Alphonso. The wealth of that one city   5
    Will make the enemy glorious.
1 Colonel.   They dare
    Not plunder it.
Alphonso.   They give fair quarter yet,
    They only seal up men's estates, and keep
    Possession for the city's use; they take up
    No wares without security, and he   10
    Whose single credit will not pass, puts in
    Two lean comrades, upon whose bonds 'tis not
    Religion to deny 'em.
Columbo.   To repair this

6–7. They ... it] *Gifford; one line in Oct.*

---

  3. *So . . . secure*] soon enough to guard.
  6. *Glorious*] (i) vainglorious; (ii) splendid.
  7. *give . . . quarter*] are merciful.
  8–9. *only . . . use*] 'The occupying forces limit their measures to freezing
private assets and administering them for the public use' (Forker).
  9–10. *take . . . security*] They guarantee repayment for what they borrow.
  10–13. *he . . .'em*] Any individual whose credit is unreliable joins in a group
whose combined pledges it would be ungenerous to reject.
  12. *lean comrades*] others whose credit is not quite enough.
  upon] on the basis of.
  13. *this*] i.e. the loss of the town.

With honour, gentlemen?

Hernando.   My opinion is
    To expect awhile.

Columbo.   Your reason?

Hernando.   Till their own   15
    Surfeit betray 'em, for their soldier,
    Bred up with coarse and common bread, will show
    Such appetites on the rich cates they find,
    They will spare our swords a victory, when their own
    Riot and luxury destroys 'em.

1 Colonel.   That   20
    Will show our patience too like a fear.
    With favour of his excellence, I think
    The spoil of cities takes not off the courage,
    But doubles it on soldiers; besides,
    While we have tameness to expect, the noise   25
    Of their success and plenty will increase
    Their army.

Hernando.   'Tis considerable, we do not
    Exceed in foot or horse, our muster not
    'Bove sixteen thousand both; and the infantry
    Raw and not disciplined to act.

Alphonso.   Their hearts,   30
    But with a brave thought of their country's honour,
    Will teach 'em how to fight, had they not seen
    A sword; but we decline our own too much,
    The men are forward in their arms, and take
    The use with avarice of fame.

27. considerable,] *Oct.;* considerable; *Gifford.*

---

16. *soldier*] soldiers.
22. *with . . . excellence*] if Hernando will excuse me (for disagreeing).
25. *tameness*] lack of spirit.
noise] report.
27. *'Tis considerable,*] ambiguous punctuation; previous edd., apart from
Forker, repunctuate so that ''Tis considerable' (worthy of consideration) refers to 'Their army'. ''Tis considerable' could also introduce Hernando's
speech: 'It must be taken into account that . . .'. Since Hernando seems to be
continuing his own argument, the second reading is more likely.
31. *But with*] with only.
33. *decline our own*] undervalue our own soldiers.
34. *forward*] zealous.
34–5. *take . . . fame*] take them up in eagerness for fame.

They rise and talk privately.

Columbo.   Colonel: 35
    I do suspect you are a coward.
Hernando.   Sir!
Columbo. Or else a traitor, take your choice; no more,
    I called you to a council, sir, of war,
    Yet keep your place.
Hernando. I have worn other names.
Columbo.   Deserve 'em, such   40
    Another were enough to unsoul an army;
    Ignobly talk of patience till they drink
    And reel to death! We came to fight and force 'em
    To mend their pace; thou hast no honour in thee,
    Not enough noble blood to make a blush   45
    For thy tame eloquence.
Hernando.   My lord, I know
    My duty to a general, yet there are
    Some that have known me here; sir, I desire
    To quit my regiment.
Columbo.   You shall have licence.
    Ink and paper—   50

Enter [Servant] *with paper and standish* [*; then exit*].

1 Colonel. The general's displeased.
2 Colonel.   How is't, Hernando?
Hernando. The general has found out employment for me,
    He is writing letters back.

49–50. You . . . paper—] *Gifford; one line in Oct.*   50.1.] *Subst. Gosse; Enter
with . . . Standish. Oct.*

  35.1. They] Columbo and Hernando.

  36. *coward*] a serious accusation which could be met only by the duel which
takes place in IV.iii. See Fredson Bowers, *J.E.G.P.*, xxxvi (1937), 40–65
(p. 63).

  37. *no more*] Let's say no more of this (as l. 39 suggests); or, no more of your
cowardly advice.

  40–1. *such | Another*] another like you.

  41. *unsoul*] deprive of courage.

  42. *patience*] i.e. patiently waiting.

  42–3. *drink . . . reel*] Cf. *The Doubtful Heir*, V.iv; IV, 355 (Forker).

  44. *mend their pace*] 'take to their heels' (Brooke).

  50.1 standish] a stand with ink, pens and writing materials.

Alphonso. ⎫
[*1*] *Captain.* ⎰　　　To his mistress?

Hernando. Pray do not trouble me, yet prithee speak,
　　　And flatter not thy friend, dost think I dare　　　　55
　　　Not draw my sword and use it, when cause
　　　With honour calls to action?

Alphonso. ⎫
[*1*] *Colonel.* ⎰　　　With the most valiant man alive.

Hernando. You'll do me some displeasure in your loves,
　　　Pray, to your places.

Columbo.　　　　　　　[*To Hernando*] So,　　　　60
　　　Bear those letters to the king,
　　　It speaks my resolution before
　　　Another sun decline, to charge the enemy.

Hernando. [*Aside*] A pretty court way
　　　Of dismissing an officer—[*To Columbo*] I obey; success　　　65
　　　Attend your counsels.　　　　　　　　　*Exit.*

Columbo. If here be any dare not look on danger,
　　　And meet it like a man with scorn of death,
　　　I beg his absence, and a coward's fear
　　　Consume him to a ghost.

1 Colonel.　　　　　　　　None such here.　　　　70

Columbo. Or if in all your regiments you find
　　　One man that does not ask to bleed with honour,

---

53. *Alphonso.* [*1*] *Captain.*] *Baskervill; Al Cap. Oct.; Alph.
Walley.* mistress?] *Gifford;* Mistress. *Oct.*　54. speak,] *Corr. Oct.;* speak.
uncorr. Oct.　58. *Alphonso.* [*1*] *Colonel.*] *Gifford; Al. Colo. Oct.*　60. *To
Hernando*] *Forker; not in Oct.*　60-1. So ... king,] *Oct.; one line in
Gifford.*　64. *Aside*] *Neilson; not in Oct.*

---

53. *mistress?*] Hernando's 'Pray do not trouble me' seems a response to
bothersome questioning and not to the plain statement of Oct., but possibly
his words preface the request for a character reference: 'Do not ask why I
make this request'.

[*1*] Captain] an arbitrary choice; there is no discernible pattern to the
speech allocation of captains or colonels in this scene. See also l. 58.

59. *You'll . . . displeasure*] Their love may harm him if Columbo notices
their support.

62. *It*] i.e. the letters. Columbo has switched from thinking of the letters
which make up his message to thinking of the message as a single communi-
cation. See ll. 83.1 and 84.

64. *pretty*] fine, with an element of irony.
court way] Hernando speaks of the soldier, Columbo.

67-70. *If . . . ghost*] Cf. *H5*, IV.iii.35-9.

Give him a double pay to leave the army;
There's service to be done, will call the spirits
And aid of men.
1 Colonel.   You give us all new flame.   75
Columbo. I am confirmed, and you must lose no time;
The soldier that was took last night, to me
Discovered their whole strength, and that we have
A party in the town; the river that
Opens the city to the west unguarded;   80
We must this night use art and resolutions,
We cannot fall ingloriously.
1 Captain. That voice is every man's.

Enter Soldier, *and* ANTONIO *with a letter.*

Columbo. What now?
Soldier.   Letters.
Columbo.   Whence?
Soldier.   From the Duchess.
Columbo. They are welcome;   85
Meet at my tent again this evening; yet stay,
Some wine!—the Duchess' health!—[*Drinks.*] See it go
    round.
                        [*Goes aside and opens the letter.*]
Antonio. It wo' not please his excellence.
1 Colonel. The Duchess' health!   [*Drinks.*]
2 Captain. To me! More wine.   90
Antonio. The clouds are gathering, and his eyes shoot fire;
Observe what thunder follows.

83.1. ANTONIO] *Gifford; Secretary Oct. (throughout scene).*   86. *evening;*
yet] *Oct.; evening; / Yet Gifford.*   87. *Drinks.*] *Gifford; not in Oct.*   *health!*
. . . See] *This ed.; health— / See Oct.*   87.1.] *Subst. Walley; not in Oct.*   89.
Drinks.] *Gifford; not in Oct.*

---

75. *men*] The implication is that those who leave – including Hernando – are
not 'men'.
76. *confirmed*] fortified in purpose.
79. *party*] group of supporters.
79–80. *the river . . . unguarded*] that the river is unguarded. 'Discovered' is
followed by an object and by two subordinate clauses. The omission of 'is' in
the second makes the structure resemble the Latin absolute construction.
81. *resolutions*] determination.
82. *ingloriously*] without glory.
83. *voice*] opinion.
91. *eyes . . . fire*] Cf. II.iii.76–8; also *The Sisters*, II.ii; V, 374.

2 Captain. The general has but ill news, I suspect
    The Duchess sick, or else the king.
1 Captain.   Maybe
    The Cardinal.
2 Captain.   His soul has long been looked for.   95
Columbo. [*Aside*] She dares not be so insolent! It is
    The Duchess' hand; how am I shrunk in fame
    To be thus played withal? She writes and counsels,
    Under my hand to send her back a free
    Resign of all my interest to her person,   100
    Promise, or love; that there's no other way
    With safety of my honour to revisit her.
    The woman is possessed with some bold devil,
    And wants an exorcism; or I am grown
    A cheap, dull, phlegmatic fool, a post that's carved   105
    I'th' common street, and holding out my forehead
    To every scurril wit to pin disgrace
    And libels on't; [*To Antonio*] did you bring this to me,
        sir?
    My thanks shall warm your heart.   *Draws a pistol.*
Antonio.   Hold, hold, my lord.
    I know not what provokes this tempest, but   110

94–5. Maybe ... Cardinal] *Subst. Gifford; one line in Oct.*   96. *Aside*]
Brooke; not in Oct.   insolent!] *Corr. Oct.; insolent, uncorr. Oct.*   108. *To
Antonio*] *Forker; not in Oct.*

---

95. *looked for*] 'expected for judgement' (Forker).

97. *how . . . fame*] how has my reputation declined?

99. *Under my hand*] in my own handwriting.

100. *Resign*] resignation; recorded only in Shirley. See III.ii.156, *The
Coronation*, IV.ii; III, 511, *The Constant Maid*, I.ii; IV, 460.

    to] in.

102. *revisit*] return to.

103. *bold*] audacious.

105. *phlegmatic*] apathetic; a reference to the medical theory of 'humours'.
Temperament depended on which fluid (humour) was dominant in the body.
The fluids, choler, phlegm, blood, and melancholy (black choler) correspon-
ded to fire, water, air, and earth. Columbo's excess of 'fire' (ll. 91 and 140)
means he is a choleric man, despite his anger at seeming phlegmatic.

105–8. *post . . .on't*] Parts of broadside ballads were pasted on public posts
as advertisements (Hyder E. Rollins, *P.M.L.A.*, xxxiv, 1919, 258–339,
p. 325); being the subject of a ballad was considered a deep disgrace (p. 277).

106. *forehead*] probably a hint at cuckold's horns.

108. *libels*] defamatory bills.

Her grace ne'er showed more freedom from a storm
When I received this paper; if you have
A will to do an execution,
Your looks without that engine, sir, may serve.
I did not like the employment.

Columbo.   Ha, had she   115
No symptom in her eye or face, of anger,
When she gave this in charge?

Antonio.   Serene, as I
Have seen the morning rise upon the spring,
No trouble in her breath, but such a wind
As came to kiss and fan the smiling flowers.   120

Columbo. No poetry.

Antonio.   By all the truth in prose,
By honesty, and your own honour, sir,
I never saw her look more calm and gentle.

Columbo. I am too passionate, you must forgive me;
[*Aside*] I have found it out, the Duchess loves me
    dearly,   125
She expressed a trouble in her when I took
My leave, and chid me with a sullen eye;
'Tis a device to hasten my return;
Love has a thousand arts; I'll answer it
Beyond her expectation, and put   130
Her soul to a noble test; [*To them*] your patience,
    gentlemen;
The king's health will deserve a sacrifice of wine.

                         [*Goes aside to write.*]

---

116. face, of] face, of *corr. Oct.;* face of *uncorr. Oct.*   117. Serene] *In italics,
Oct.*   125. Aside] *Subst. Brooke; not in Oct.*   132.1.] *Subst. Gifford; not in
Oct.*

---

114. *engine*] offensive weapon (i.e. the pistol).

117–20. *Serene . . . flowers*] one of the few passages which counters the
play's storm imagery. The lines are characteristic of Shirley; cf. *The Brothers,*
I.i; I, 202, *The Sisters,* IV.ii; V, 399.

121. *in prose*] common in Shirley (e.g. *Hyde Park,* IV.iii; II, 514) and
elsewhere (Chapman, *Widow's Tears,* IV.i.48; Marston, *Dutch Courtesan,*
I.i.10).

128–31. *device . . . test*] Forsythe (p. 75) notes other instances of trials of
love and chastity. Here Columbo assumes he is being tested whereas he is
really being rejected. The Duchess interprets *his* testing as her release.

Antonio. [*Aside*] I am glad to see this change, and thank my
    wit
    For my redemption.
1 Colonel.   Sir,
    The soldiers' curse on him loves not our master.   135
2 Colonel. And they curse loud enough to be heard.
2 Captain. Their curse has the nature of gunpowder.
Antonio. They do not pray with half the noise.
1 Colonel. Our general is not well mixed,
    He has too great a portion of fire.   140
2 Colonel. His mistress cool him—her complexion
    Carries some phlegm—when they two meet in bed!
2 Captain. A third may follow.
1 Captain.   'Tis much pity
    The young duke lived not to take the virgin off.
1 Colonel. 'Twas the king's act to match two rabbit-suckers.   145
2 Colonel. A common trick of state;
    The little great man marries, travels then

---

133. *Aside*] *Subst. Gifford; not in Oct.*   134–5. Sir ... master] *This ed.; one
line in Oct.*   135. soldiers'] *Brooke;* Souldiers *Oct.;* soldiers *Gifford;*
soldier's *Gosse.*   141. him—her] *Walley;* him, her *Oct.*   142.
phlegm—when] *Walley;* phlegm, when *Oct.* bed!] *Gifford;* bed? *Oct.*   143.
pity /] *Gifford;* pity./ *Oct.*

---

135. *soldiers' curse*] Gifford, presumably influenced by l. 136, takes 'curse'
as a verb. Other edd. treat 'curse' as a noun. Although 'soldier's' (Gosse) and
'soldiers'' (Brooke) are both possible, the latter seems more likely, given
'they' in l. 136.

139–40. *not . . . fire*] See note on l. 105.

141. *complexion*] disposition.

141–2. *cool . . . phlegm*] Phlegm was linked with water and was cold and
moist, whereas choler (fire) was hot and dry. Columbo and his mistress are
opposites.

143. *A third*] They may have a child.

'*Tis much pity*/] The pity lies in what follows and is not a comment on what
goes before.

144. *take . . . off*] deflower.

145. *rabbit-suckers*] orig. a sucking-rabbit; from 1608 (*O.E.D.*, 2), young
innocents.

146. *trick of state*] foolish act (*O.E.D.*, 2b), of princes (*O.E.D.*, 24).

147–50.] See Stone, pp. 618–19 and 652–60, for an account of the betrothal
and marriage of children, sometimes followed by a token consummation and
then the Grand Tour for the young man. The Duchess's match resembles a
recent 'unlucky' marriage. In 1626 Charles, seven-year-old son of the Earl of
Montgomery, was betrothed to the Duke of Buckingham's four-year-old

Till both grow up, and dies when he should do
The feat; these things are still unlucky
On the male side.   150
Columbo. This to the Duchess' fair hand.

                      [*Gives Antonio a letter.*]
Antonio.   She will think
Time hath no wing, till I return.   [*Exit.*]
Columbo.   Gentlemen,
Now each man to his quarter, and encourage
The soldier; I shall take a pride to know
Your diligence, when I visit all   155
Your several commands.
Omnes.   We shall expect.
2 Colonel. And move by your directions.
Columbo.   Y'are all noble.

                    Exeunt.

ACT II, SCENE ii

Enter CARDINAL, DUCHESS, PLACENTIA.

Cardinal. I shall perform a visit daily, madam,
In th'absence of my nephew, and be happy
If you accept my care.
Duchess.   You have honoured me,
And if your entertainment have not been
Worthy your grace's person, 'tis because   5
Nothing can reach it in my power; but where
There is no want of zeal, other defect
Is only a fault to exercise your mercy.

---

151. *Gives Antonio a letter.*] *Gifford; not in Oct.*   152. *Exit.*] *Gifford; not in Oct.*   155-6. all/ Your] *This ed.;* all your / Severall *Oct.;* all your several / *Gifford.*

---

daughter. They were married in 1635 but within a year Charles died on the Grand Tour and his father had to repay the bride's dowry (Stone, pp. 618–19).

    149. *still*] always.

    152. *Time . . . wing*] another favourite image; cf. *The Bird in a Cage,* I.i; II, 373, *The Example,* IV.i; III, 333.

    4. *entertainment*] way you have been received. Note the superficial politeness.

    8. *fault . . . mercy*] a fault whose only function is to exercise your mercy.

Cardinal. You are bounteous in all; I take my leave,
  My fair niece, shortly, when Columbo has   10
  Purchased more honours to prefer his name
  And value to your noble thoughts; meantime
  Be confident you have a friend, whose office
  And favour with the king shall be effectual
  To serve your grace.
Duchess.   Your own good deeds reward you,   15
  Till mine rise equal to deserve their benefit.

                                        Exit CARDINAL.

  Leave me awhile.

                                        Exit PLACENTIA.

  Do not I walk upon the teeth of serpents;
  And, as I had a charm against their poison,
  Play with their stings? The Cardinal is subtle,   20
  Whom 'tis not wisdom to incense, till I
  Hear to what destiny Columbo leaves me;
  Maybe the greatness of his soul will scorn
  To own what comes with murmur, if he can
  Interpret me so happily;

                    Enter ANTONIO *with a letter.*

                              art come?   25
Antonio. His excellence salutes your grace.
Duchess.   Thou hast
  A melancholy brow; how did he take my letter?
Antonio. As he would take a blow, with so much sense
  Of anger, his whole soul boiled in his face,
  And such prodigious flame in both his eyes   30
  As they'd been th'only seat of fire; and at

9. leave,] *Gifford;* leave; *Oct.*   20. stings? ... subtle,] *Gifford;* stings, ...
subtle? *Oct.*   25.1.] *After* happily; *Forker; after* come? *Oct.*   ANTONIO]
Gifford; Secretary *Oct. (throughout scene).*

9–10. *leave ... shortly*] Oct.'s punctuation is awkward. If we accept
Gifford's change we must read 'my fair niece, as you will shortly be'.
  11. *Purchased*] earned.
  prefer] exalt.
  15–16. *Your ... benefit*] May your own good deeds reward you until, by
equalling you in generosity, I become worthy of your kindness.
  23. *greatness of his soul*] i.e. his noble soul.
  24. *with murmur*] discontentedly.
  24–5. *if ... happily*] if I am fortunate enough to be so understood.

Each look a salamander leaping forth,
Not able to endure the furnace.
Duchess.   Ha! Thou dost
Describe him with some horror.
Antonio.   Soon as he
Had read again, and understood your meaning,   35
His rage had shot me with a pistol, had not
I used some soft and penitential language,
To charm the bullet.
Duchess.   Wait at some more distance;
                              [*Antonio goes aside.*]
My soul doth bathe itself in a cold dew;
Imagine I am opening of a tomb,   [*Opens the letter.*]   40
Thus I throw off the marble to discover
What antic posture death presents in this
Pale monument to fright me—   *Reads.*
Ha! My heart, that called my blood and spirits to
Defend it from the invasion of my fears,   45
Must keep a guard about it still, lest this
Strange and too mighty joy crush it to nothing.
Antonio.
Antonio.   Madam.
Duchess.   Bid my steward give thee
Two thousand ducats; art sure I am awake?
Antonio. I shall be able to resolve you, madam,   50
When he has paid the money.
Duchess. Columbo now is noble.   *Exit* DUCHESS.

---

32. salamander] *In italics, Oct.*   38.1.] *Subst. Forker; not in Oct.*   39.
bathe] *Gifford;* bath *Oct.*   40. *Opens the letter.*] *Gifford; not in Oct.*

---

32. *salamander*] lizard-like animal, supposed to be able to endure fire.
39. *bathe*] Oct.'s 'bath' was a verb in its own right and also a variant spelling
of 'bathe'. 'Bath' differs from 'bathe' in referring more distinctly to a bath-
tub. Since the Duchess describes perspiration flowing over the body, the
more figurative 'bathe' seems appropriate.
42. *antic*] Shakespeare associates both noun (*R2*, III.ii.162) and adjective
(*1H6*, IV.vii.18) with death.
43. *monument*] sepulchre, tomb.
49. *Two thousand ducats*] The ducat varied in value but even the lowest sum
mentioned in *O.E.D.* (*c.* seventeen pence) makes the reward huge by the
standards of the 1640s. Although Antonio's reaction suggests the reward is
greater than he expected, I suspect 'ducat' is used loosely to mean 'coin'.

Antonio.   This is better
    Than I expected, if my lady be
    Not mad, and live to justify her bounty.   *Exit.*

                    ACT II, Scene iii

            Enter KING, ALVAREZ, HERNANDO, Lords.

King. The war is left to him, but we must have
    You reconciled, if that be all your difference.
    His rage flows like a torrent when he meets
    With opposition; leave to wrestle with him,
    And his hot blood retreats into a calm,   5
    And then he chides his passion; you shall back
    With letters from us.
Antonio.   Your commands are not
    To be disputed.
King.   Alvarez.   [*Takes him aside.*]
1 Lord.   [*To Hernando*] Lose not
    Yourself by cool submission; he will find
    His error, and the want of such a soldier.   10
2 Lord. Have you seen the Cardinal?
Hernando.   Not yet.
1 Lord. He wants no plot—
Hernando.   The king I must obey;
    But let the purple gownman place his engines
    I'th' dark that wounds me.

52–3. This . . . be] *Gifford; one line in Oct.*   8. *Takes him aside.*] *Gifford; not in Oct.   To Hernando*] *Forker; not in Oct.*   14. dark that wounds] *Oct.;* dark, that wound *Gifford;* dark; that wounds *Forker.*

---

54. *Not mad*] Antonio anticipates the Duchess's later madness.

    1. *The . . . him*] Columbo has the final say in the war's strategy.
    2. *that*] i.e. their quarrel over strategy.
    4. *leave to wrestle*] stop wrestling.
    6. *back*] go back.
    13–14. *But . . . me*] either 'Let the Cardinal, who is out to wound me, lay his weapons ('engines') in dark places (if he wants to get away with it)' or, 'let the Cardinal lay in dark places the weapons that will wound me'. The latter is marginally more likely. See Abbott § 333 for third person plural in *-s.* Cf. *Chabot,* V.iii, 'The engine is not seen that wounds thy master' (Gifford, VI, 160; in a scene probably by Chapman but revised by Shirley). Forker's punctuation seems unnecessarily complicated.

2 Lord.   Be assured
  Of what we can to friend you, and the king   15
  Cannot forget your service.
Hernando.   I am sorry
  For that poor gentleman.
Alvarez.   [*To the King*] I must confess, sir,
  The Duchess has been pleased to think me worthy
  Her favours, and in that degree of honour
  That has obliged my life to make the best   20
  Return of service, which is not, with bold
  Affiance in her love, to interpose
  Against her happiness and your election;
  I love so much her honour, I have quitted
  All my desires, yet would not shrink to bleed   25
  Out my warm stock of life, so the last drop
  Might benefit her wishes.
King.   I shall find
  A compensation for this act, Alvarez,
  It hath much pleased us.

        Enter DUCHESS *with a letter*, Gentleman-Usher.

Duchess.   Sir, you are the king,
  And in that sacred title it were sin   30
  To doubt a justice; all that does concern
  My essence in this world, and a great part
  Of the other bliss, lives in your breath.
King. What intends the Duchess?
Duchess. [*Giving him the letter*] That will instruct you, sir;

17. *To the King*] *Forker; not in* Oct.   33. your] *Gifford;* you Oct.   35.
Giving him the letter] *Subst. Gifford; not in* Oct.

---

   15. *Of . . . you*] of any help we can give you.
   17. *that . . . gentleman*] i.e. Alvarez.
   19–23. *and . . . election*] and she has honoured me so much that she has obliged me to do the best I can for her; so I shall not with bold confidence in her love interfere in her happiness and your choice of her husband.
   24. *quitted*] renounced.
   27–8. *find | A compensation*] reward you.
   30. *sacred title*] a reference to the divine right of kings, a theory especially associated with the Stuarts whose rights were under attack in the Puritan campaign against Charles I and his advisers.
   32. *essence*] life.
   33. *other bliss*] the bliss of the other world. See I.ii.82.
   lives in your breath] depends on what you say.

   Columbo has,   35
  Upon some better choice, or discontent,
  Set my poor soul at freedom.
King.   'Tis his character— *Reads.*
  'Madam, I easily discharge all my pretensions to your love
  and person; I leave you to your own choice, and in what
  you have obliged yourself to me, resume a power to cancel 40
  if you please.   Columbo.'
  This is strange.
Duchess.   Now do an act to make
  Your chronicle beloved and read for ever.
King. Express yourself.
Duchess.   Since by divine infusion,
  For 'tis no art could force the general to   45
  This change, second this justice and bestow
  The heart you would have given from me, by
  Your strict commands to love Columbo, where
  'Twas meant by heaven, and let your breath return
  Whom you divorced, Alvarez, mine.
Lords.   This is   50
  But justice, sir.
King.   It was decreed above,
  And since Columbo has released his interest
  Which we had wrought him, not without some force

38–41. *As prose*] *All modern edd.; as verse and in italics* Oct. (. . . *pretensions* / . . .
to your / . . . *obliged* / . . . *cancell* / . . . *please*). 38. pretensions] *pretensions corr.*
Oct.; *pretentions uncorr.* Oct. 39. what] *what corr.* Oct.; *weat uncorr.*
Oct. 50–1. This . . . sir] *Gifford; one line in* Oct. 53–4. force / Upon your
will, I] *Gifford;* force / Upon your will I *Oct.;* force, / Upon your will I *Forker.*

 36.] either because he has found a better match or because he is dissatisfied
with me.
 37. *character*] handwriting.
 38. *easily*] freely.
 discharge . . . *pretensions*] give up claims.
 39–40. *in what* . . . *me*] as for our engagement.
 43. *chronicle*] record of your reign.
 44. *Since* . . . *infusion*] The Duchess does not complete her sentence but is
diverted by another thought. We must understand 'since divine influence has
led Columbo to release me . . .'.
 49–50. *Let* . . . *mine*] Let your voice restore to me Alvarez, whom you
parted from me. Verb – 'return' – and object – 'Alvarez' – are separated by a
relative clause; characteristic of Shirley's syntax (Bas, p. 386).
 52–4. *since* . . . *.wishes*] Oct.'s punctuation is ambiguous. Forker's suggests a

Upon your will, I give you your own wishes,
Receive your own Alvarez; when you please   55
To celebrate your nuptial, I invite
Myself your guest.
Duchess.   Eternal blessings crown you.
Omnes. And every joy your marriage.

     [*As* KING *exits, he*] *meets the* CARDINAL; *they confer.*

Alvarez. I know not whether I shall wonder most,
   Or joy to meet this happiness.
Duchess.   Now the king   60
Hath planted us, methinks we grow already,
And twist our loving souls above the wrath
Of thunder to divide us.
Alvarez.   Ha! The Cardinal
Has met the king, I do not like this conference;
He looks with anger this way, I expect   65
A tempest.
Duchess.   Take no notice of his presence,
Leave me to meet and answer it; if the king
Be firm in's royal word, I fear no lightning;
Expect me in the garden.
Alvarez.   I obey,
But fear a shipwreck on the coast.   *Exit.*   70

[*Exit* KING, *followed by* HERNANDO, Lords, Gentleman-Usher.]

58.1. *As* KING *exits, he*] *Subst. Gifford; Exit King, who Oct.*   60–3. Now . . .
king / Hath . . . already, / And . . . wrath / Of] *Gifford;* Now . . . us / Methinks
. . . souls / Above . . . *Oct.*   70.1.] *This ed.; not in Oct.; Exeunt D'Alvarez,
Hernando . . . Gentleman-Usher. Lawrence.*

---

hitherto unmentioned reluctance in Columbo; Gifford's stresses the
Duchess's reluctance and accords better with what we are told: 'Since
Columbo has relinquished his claim, which we had persuaded him to against
your desire, I give you your own wishes.'

   58.1.] Presumably Hernando and the courtiers follow the king, leaving
Alvarez and the Duchess alone. It is unlikely that the king's followers would
leave before him. They stand aside while he confers with the Cardinal.

   62. *twist*] could also = 'copulate' (Marston, *Fawn*, IV.i.312); the image thus
implies spiritual *and* physical union.

   64. *I . . . conference*] See *The Royal Master*, I.i: 'I do not like their conference' (IV, 108).

   70.1] an appropriate moment for the king's exit. As Alvarez leaves through
one door (to the garden, l. 70), the king and his entourage depart through the
other, leaving the Cardinal to confront the Duchess.

Cardinal. Madam.

Duchess. My lord.

Cardinal. The king speaks of a letter that has brought
     A riddle in't.

Duchess.   'Tis easy to interpret.

Cardinal. From my nephew? May I deserve the favour?
                         [*Duchess gives him the letter*.]   75

Duchess. [*Aside*] He looks as though his eyes would fire the
          paper.
     They are a pair of burning glasses, and
     His envious blood doth give 'em flame.

Cardinal. [*Aside*] What lethargy could thus unspirit him?
     I am all wonder; [*To her*] do not believe, madam,   80
     But that Columbo's love is yet more sacred
     To honour and yourself, than thus to forfeit
     What I have heard him call the glorious wreath
     To all his merits, given him by the king,
     From whom he took you with more pride than ever   85
     He came from victory; his kisses hang
     Yet panting on your lips, and he but now
     Exchanged religious farewell to return
     But with more triumph to be yours.

Duchess.   My lord,
     You do believe your nephew's hand was not   90
     Surprised or strained to this?

Cardinal. Strange arts and windings in the world, most dark,
     And subtle progresses; who brought this letter?

---

75. *Duchess gives him the letter*.] *Gifford; not in Oct.*   76. *Aside*] *Neilson; not
in Oct.*   79. *Aside*] *Subst. Gifford; not in Oct.*

71–168.] For the resemblance to *H8*, see Introduction, n.22.

75. *May . . . favour?*] May I read the letter?

76–8. *fire . . . burning . . . flame*] The imagery links the Cardinal with his
nephew (see II.i.91).

77. *burning glasses*] lenses which focus the sun's rays and start a fire with the
heat. Cf. *The Maid's Revenge*, III.i; I, 135.

78. *envious*] malicious.

82. *than thus*] than that he would thus.

87–8. *he . . . return*] he recently (*O.E.D.*, Now, adv., 3) bade you a devoted
farewell and promised to return. Cf. Forker: he 'devotedly took leave (of his
men at the front)'.

89. *But with*] with even.

91. *Surprised or strained*] taken by sudden assault or superior force.

Duchess. I enquired not his name, I thought it not
    Considerable to take such narrow knowledge.   95
Cardinal. Desert and honour urged it here, nor can
    I blame you to be angry; yet his person
    Obliged you should have given a nobler pause,
    Before you made your faith and change so violent
    From his known worth, into the arms of one,   100
    However fashioned to your amorous wish,
    Not equal to his cheapest fame, with all
    The gloss of blood and merit.
Duchess.   This comparison,
    My good lord Cardinal, I cannot think
    Flows from an even justice; it betrays   105
    You partial where your blood runs.
Cardinal.   I fear, madam,
    Your own takes too much licence, and will soon
    Fall to the censure of unruly tongues;
    Because Alvarez has a softer cheek,
    Can like a woman trim his wanton hair,   110
    Spend half a day with looking in the glass
    To find a posture to present himself,
    And bring more effeminacy than man
    Or honour to your bed; must he supplant him?
    Take heed, the common murmur when it catches   115
    The scent of a lost fame—

94–5.] I did not think it important enough to ask for such precise information. Gifford finds the lines awkward but the meaning and the sarcasm are
clear enough. The encounter gains edge from the desire of both combatants to
wound (ll. 101, 106, 107).

96. *Desert*] i.e. Columbo's.

98. *Obliged*] 'put you under obligation' (Brooke).

nobler] more fitting his dignity.

99. *faith and change*] 'change of faith' (Forker).

102–3. *Not equal . . . merit*] of less worth than even the lowest estimation of
Columbo's reputation, which is enhanced by his birth and his deserts.

105. *even*] impartial.

106. *where . . . runs*] to your blood relations.

107. *Your . . . licence*] The Cardinal twists the sense of blood so that it
refers not to kindred but to passion.

110. *wanton*] luxuriant, with pejorative overtones.

112. *posture*] pose. 'Posture' implies affectation and was frequently associated with courtiers.

113. *man*] manliness.

114. *him*] i.e. Columbo.

Duchess.   My fame, lord Cardinal?
    It stands upon an innocence as clear
    As the devotions you pay to heaven;
    I shall not urge, my lord, your soft indulgence
    At my next shrift.
Cardinal.   You are a fine court lady.   120
Duchess. And you should be a reverend churchman.
Cardinal.   One,
    That if you have not thrown off modesty
    Would counsel you to leave Alvarez.
Duchess.   'Cause
    You dare do worse than marriage, must not I
    Be admitted what the church and law allows me?   125
Cardinal. Insolent! Then you dare marry him?
Duchess.   Dare!
    Let your contracted flame and malice, with
    Columbo's rage higher than that, meet us
    When we approach the holy place, clasped hand
    In hand; we'll break through all your force and fix   130
    Our sacred vows together there.
Cardinal.   I knew
    When with as chaste a brow you promised fair

121–2. One ... modesty] *Gifford; one line in Oct.*   123–5. 'Cause / You ... I /
Be] *Gifford;* Cause ... worse / Than ... what / The *Oct.*   126–7. Dare ...
with] *Gifford; one line in Oct.*   130. hand; we'll] *Forker;* hand, wee'l *Oct.;*
hand we'll *Neilson;* hand: we'll *Brooke.*

  119–20. *I shall . . . shrift*] I shall not press for your pardon when I next
confess.

  119. *soft*] easy; an ironic reference to the Cardinal's gentleness with (presumably) high-born sinners.

  indulgence] remission of punishment after absolution.

  121. *reverend*] The Duchess lays stress on the original meaning, 'worthy of
respect', of a term conventionally used in addressing churchmen.

  124. *dare do worse*] The Cardinal as a celibate priest should find his pleasure
on a spiritual level above that of earthly marriage. The Duchess implies that
he seeks grosser pleasures and foreshadows his behaviour in V.iii.

  127. *contracted*] Perhaps 'united'; 'contracted flame and malice' would then
mean 'burning ill-will' (cf. *The Imposture*, III.iii; V, 224). Or perhaps the
Cardinal's rage is 'shrunken' (i.e. mean-minded) in contrast to Columbo's
'higher' rage.

  129–30. *When . . . break*] Oct.'s syntax is ambiguous. Either the Duchess
means, 'meet us when we approach the holy place with hands clasped; then
we'll break . . .' or, 'meet us when we approach the holy place; with clasped
hands we'll break . . .'. The former is more likely.

To another; you are no dissembling lady.
Duchess. Would all your actions had no falser lights
    About 'em.   135
Cardinal. Ha?
Duchess. The people would not talk and curse so loud.
Cardinal. I'll have you chid into a blush for this.
Duchess. Begin at home, great man, there's cause enough;
    You turn the wrong end of the perspective   140
    Upon your crimes, to drive them to a far
    And lesser sight, but let your eyes look right,
    What giants would your pride and surfeit seem!
    How gross your avarice, eating up whole families!
    How vast are your corruptions and abuse   145
    Of the king's ear! At which you hang a pendant,
    Not to adorn, but ulcerate, while the honest
    Nobility, like pictures in the arras,
    Serve only for court-ornament; if they speak,
    'Tis when you set their tongues, which you wind up   150
    Like clocks, to strike at the just hour you please;
    Leave, leave, my lord, these usurpations,
    And be what you were meant, a man to cure,
    Not let in agues to religion;
    Look on the church's wounds.
Cardinal.   You dare presume   155
    In your rude spleen to me, to abuse the church?
Duchess. Alas, you give false aim, my lord, 'tis your

137. talk and] *Oct.;* talk, and *Gifford.*

---

133. *you . . . lady*] a stock piece of irony.
134–5.] I wish your actions were no more deceitful than mine.
137. *The people*] an 'allusion to the growing religious discontent in 1641' (Forker).
139. *at home*] i.e. with yourself.
140. *perspective*] telescope; 'looking through the wrong end of a perspective', first recorded figuratively in 1646 (*O.E.D.*, Perspective, sb., 2).
141–2. *far . . . sight*] See IV.ii.222–6, where the Cardinal is again accused of blurring events and words by keeping them at a distance.
142. *let . . . right*] if you look through it the right way.
145. *How vast . . . corruptions*] an allusion to Laud? (Boas, p. 376).
146. *pendant*] earring, something which hangs on. Cf. *The Politician*, I.i; V, 96.
148. *pictures . . . arras*] pictures in a hanging tapestry. See Massinger, *The Duke of Milan*, II.i.93: 'Arras pictures of Nobilitie' (*Plays*, I, 240).
151. *just*] exact.

      Ambition and scarlet sins that rob
      Her altar of the glory, and leave wounds
      Upon her brow; which fetches grief and paleness   160
      Into her cheeks; making her troubled bosom
      Pant with her groans, and shroud her holy blushes
      Within your reverend purples.
Cardinal.   Will you now take breath?
Duchess. In hope, my lord, you will behold yourself
      In a true glass, and see those injust acts   165
      That so deform you, and by timely cure
      Prevent a shame, before the short-haired men
      Do crowd and call for justice. I take leave.   *Exit.*
Cardinal. This woman has a spirit that may rise
      To tame the devil's; there's no dealing with   170
      Her angry tongue, 'tis action and revenge
      Must calm her fury; were Columbo here,
      I could resolve, but letters shall be sent
      To th'army which may wake him into sense
      Of his rash folly, or direct his spirit   175
      Some way to snatch his honour from this flame;
      All great men know, *the soul of life is fame.*   *Exit.*

---

170. devil's] *Gifford;* Devils *Oct.*

---

   158. *scarlet sins*] another reference to the Cardinal's clothing. See also l.
163, and Heywood's *Woman Killed with Kindness*, xiii.46.
   162. *shroud*] seek shelter for. Cf. *Duchess of Malfi*, I.i.502, and *Changeling*,
III.iv.167 (Forker).
   164–8.] probably 'I take breath in hope . . .' but just possibly 'I take leave'
is the main clause; if so, l. 168 should read 'justice – I take leave'.
   165. *true glass*] one which does not distort.
   167. *short-haired men*] a scornful reference to the Puritans. See Lucy Hutchinson, *Memoirs of the Life of Colonel Hutchinson*, ed. James Sutherland
(London, 1973), p. 63: 'few of the Puritanes . . . wore their hair long enough
to cover their eares, and the ministers and many others cut it close round their
heads, with so many little peakes as was something ridiculous to behold.'
   170. *devil's*] Oct. is ambiguous. Most edd. punctuate with an apostrophe
thus making the Cardinal refer to the devil's spirit, but 'devils', if less likely, is
not impossible.
   177. the . . . fame] Underlining frequently marks gnomic utterances in
seventeenth-century texts. Cf. V.i.99, V.iii.297.

Act III

ACT III, Scene i

Enter VALERIA, CELINDA.

Valeria. I did not think, Celinda, when I praised
    Alvarez to the Duchess, that things thus
    Would come about. What does your ladyship
    Think of Columbo now? It staggers all
    The court, he should forsake his mistress; I   5
    Am lost with wonder yet.
Celinda.   'Tis very strange
    Without a spell; but there's a fate in love,
    I like him ne'er the worse.

Enter two Lords.

1 Lord. Nothing but marriages and triumph now.
Valeria. What new access of joy makes you, my lord,   10
    So pleasant?
1 Lord.   There's a packet come to court
    Makes the king merry, we are all concerned in't.
    Columbo hath given the enemy a great
    And glorious defeat, and is already
    Preparing to march home.   15
Celinda. He thrived the better for my prayers.
2 Lord. You have been his great admirer, madam.
1 Lord. The king longs to see him.
Valeria. This news exalts the Cardinal.

Enter CARDINAL.

---

7. *Without a spell*] unless a charm has been used on him.
9. *triumph*] public celebrations.
11. *packet*] i.e. of letters.
19. *exalts*] elates.
19.1.] The Cardinal remains meditating in the background.

86

1 Lord.   He's here,
    He appears with discontent, the marriage   20
    With Count D'Alvarez hath a bitter taste,
    And not worn off his palate; but let us leave him.
Ladies. We'll to the Duchess.
            Exeunt [VALERIA, CELINDA, Lords]*; manet* CARDINAL.

Cardinal. He has not won so much upon the Aragon
    As he has lost at home, and his neglect   25
    Of what my studies had contrived, to add
    More lustre to our family by the access
    Of the great Duchess' fortune, cools his triumph,
    And makes me wild.

                    Enter HERNANDO.

Hernando.   My good lord Cardinal.
Cardinal. You made complaint to th' king about your
            general.   30
Hernando. Not a complaint, my lord, I did but satisfy
    Some questions o' the king's.
Cardinal.   You see he thrives
    Without your personal valour or advice,
    Most grave and learned in the wars.
Hernando.   My lord,
    I envy not his fortune.
Cardinal.   'Tis above   35
    Your malice, and your noise not worth his anger,
    'Tis barking 'gainst the moon.
Hernando.   More temper would
    Become that habit.
Cardinal. The military thing would show some spleen;

23.1.] *Subst. Walley; Exeunt. manet Car. Oct.*

---

22. *And not*] and hath not.
23.1. *manet*] remains.
24. *upon the Aragon*] from the Aragonians.
25–6. *neglect . . . contrived*] disregard of what I had planned.
29. *wild*] furious.
34. *Most . . . wars*] sneeringly addressed to Hernando.
36. *noise*] slander.
37. *barking . . . moon*] proverbial; Tilley, M1119.
38. *habit*] cardinal's dress.

D

I'll blow an army of such wasps about   40
The world; go look your sting you left i'th' camp, sir.

Enter KING, *and* Lords.

Hernando. The king. This may be one day counted for. *Exit.*
King. All things conspire, my lord, to make you fortunate,
  Your nephew's glory—
Cardinal.   'Twas your cause and justice
  Made him victorious; had he been so valiant   45
  At home, he had had another conquest to
  Invite and bid her welcome to new wars.
King. You must be reconciled to providence, my lord;
  I heard you had a controversy with
  The Duchess, I will have you friends.   50
Cardinal. I am not angry.
King.   For my sake then
  You shall be pleased, and with me grace the marriage;
  A churchman must show charity, and shine
  With first example; she's a woman.
Cardinal. You shall prescribe in all things; sir, you cannot 55
  Accuse my love, if I still wish my nephew
  Had been so happy to be constant to
  Your own and my election; yet my brain
  Cannot reach how this comes about; I know
  My nephew loved her with a near affection.   60

Enter HERNANDO.

42.] *Subst. Gifford;* King. *Exit.* / This . . . for. *Oct.*   51–2. For . . . marriage;]
Subst. Gifford; For . . . pleas'd, / And . . . Mariage; *Oct.*   55. things; sir,]
Oct.; things, sir. *Gifford.*

40–1. *I'll . . . world*] I'm capable of scattering a host of insects like you all
over the world.
  41. *Look . . . sting*] Look for your sting. The Cardinal implies that
Hernando is now harmless. Cf. II.i.75n.
  42. *counted*] accounted.
  44. *your cause and justice*] 'the justice of your cause' (Forker).
  45–7. *had . . . wars*] If Columbo had fought so hard for the Duchess, he
could have conquered her and then invited and welcomed her to the amorous
wars of marriage.
  56. *Accuse my love*] 'accuse me of wavering in my love to you' (Forker) or
perhaps, 'blame my love (for my nephew)'.
  59. *reach*] understand.

King. He'll give you fair account at his return.

    [*To Hernando*] Colonel, your letters may be spared, the
      general

    Has finished, and is coming home.

Hernando. I am glad on't, sir.

                                [*Exit* KING.]

                  My good lord Cardinal!

    [*Aside*] 'Tis not impossible but some man provoked   65

    May have a precious mind to cut your throat.

Cardinal. You shall command me, noble colonel;

    I know you wo' not fail to be at th'wedding.

Hernando. 'Tis not Columbo that is married, sir.

Cardinal. Go teach the postures of the pike and musket,   70

    Then drill your myrmidons into a ditch,

    Where starve, and stink in pickle; you shall find

    Me reasonable; you see the king expects me.

Hernando [*Aside*] So does the devil; some desperate hand

    May help you on your journey.   *Exeunt.*   75

---

62. *To Hernando*] *Forker; not in Oct.*   64.1.] *Subst. Gifford; not in
Oct.*   74. *Aside*] *Forker; not in Oct.*   So ... hand /] *Oct.;* So ... devil.—/
Some *Gifford.*   75. *Exeunt.*] *Oct.; Gifford provides separate exits after the last
two speeches.*

---

  65. *but*] but that.

  66. *precious mind*] strong desire.

  70. *postures*] positions of weapon in drill.

  71. *myrmidons*] faithful followers; ruffians (Lawrence). The Myrmidons
were Achilles' Thessalian troops.

  72. *starve*] die. The mood is optative subjunctive, the person ambiguous;
the Cardinal probably means 'May you starve' (Forker). Or possibly, after the
commands in ll. 70–1, 'starve' has imperative force.

  pickle] disagreeable situation, or a picturesque description of the contents
of the ditch.

  72–3. *you . . . reasonable*] possibly with heavy irony, 'then you will find me
ready to listen to reason' or, 'you shall find that I behave sensibly at the
wedding' (l. 68).

  74. *So . . . devil*] Cf. V.iii.54.

ACT III, Scene ii

Enter ANTONIO *and* Servants[, *including* PEDRO *and* JAQUES].

Antonio. [*Handing out costumes*] Here this, ay this will fit your
    part; you shall wear the slashes, because you are a soldier;
    here's for the blue mute.

1 Servant. This doublet will never fit me, pox on't, are these
    breeches good enough for a prince too? Pedro plays but a   5
    lord, and he has two laces more in a seam.

Antonio. You must consider Pedro is a foolish lord, he may
    wear what lace he please.

2 Servant. Does my beard fit my clothes well, gentlemen?

Antonio. Pox o' your beard.   10

3 Servant. That will fright away the hair.

1 Servant. This fellow plays but a mute, and he is so
    troublesome, and talks.

0.1 ANTONIO] *Gifford; Secretary Oct. (throughout scene).   including* PEDRO
and JAQUES] *Subst. Forker; not in Oct.*   1. *Handing out costumes*] *Subst.
Forker; not in Oct.*

    0.1.] The servants' identities are not clearly established. 5 Servant, who
enters looking for a 'head' (l. 26), is Rogero (l. 65). In l. 29 Antonio asks if
Jaques has the head, and the response shows that 4 Servant is Jaques. Both 1
Servant and 3 Servant refer to Pedro. But if we look at 2 Servant we discover
that he plays a 'blue mute' (l. 18), a non-speaking servant role, whereas Pedro
is a 'foolish lord' (l. 7). Forker believes the mute is confusingly given lines, but
his evidence is inconclusive (see l. 54n). Either Pedro does not speak and is
merely seen breaking buttons (Forker) or Shirley had not straightened out the
servants' identities in his manuscript.
    1. *Handing out costumes*] See *M.N.D.*, I.ii, where parts in a play are al-
located and costumes discussed. Chapman's *Gentleman Usher*, II.i, is a possible source (Forsythe; see his pp. 187–8 for similar scenes). The comic scene
provides the only prose in *The Cardinal* apart from the letters.
    2. *slashes*] (i) slit in a garment to expose lining; (ii) a wound.
    3. *blue*] the colour worn by servants; see M. Channing Linthicum, *Costume
in the Drama of Shakespeare and his Contemporaries* (Oxford, 1936), p. 27.
    4. *pox on't*] a plague on it. The 'plague' is syphilis.
    6. *two laces more*] a reference to the braid laces used for fastening garments.
By 1640 these were largely decorative (Doreen Yarwood, *English Costume*,
London, 1952, pp. 147–9). The comment suggests that more laces went with
higher rank.
    9. *gentlemen*] the servants' term of address throughout this scene (ll. 26, 31,
68, 74, 80); perhaps a courtly affectation.
    11.] a familiar joke, taking 'pox' literally; loss of hair was a symptom of
syphilis.

3 Servant. Master secretary might have let Jaques play the
    soldier, he has a black patch already.   15
2 Servant. By your favour, master secretary, I was asked who
    writ this play for us.
Antonio. For us? Why, art thou any more than a blue mute?
2 Servant. And by my troth, I said I thought it was all your
    own.   20
Antonio. Away, you coxcomb.
4 Servant. [*Jaques.*] Dost think he has no more wit than to write
    a comedy? My lady's chaplain made the play, though he is
    content, for the honour and trouble of the business, to be
    seen in't.   25

Enter Fifth Servant [ROGERO].

Rogero. Did anybody see my head, gentlemen? 'Twas here but
    now. I shall have never a head to play my part in.
Antonio. Is thy head gone? 'Tis well thy part was not in't; look,
    look about, has not Jaques it?
Jaques. I his head? 'T wo' not come on upon my shoulders.   30
Antonio. Make haste, gentlemen, I'll see whether the king has
    supped; look every man to his wardrobe and his part.
                              Exit [*with* ROGERO.]

15. black patch] *Corr. Oct.;* plack batch *uncorr. Oct.*   22. *Jaques.*] *Forker;* 4
Oct. (throughout scene).   25.1. ROGERO] *Forker;* 5th. Servant *Oct. (throughout scene).*   32. *with* ROGERO] *Subst. Baskervill; not in Oct.*

---

15. *black patch*] presumably an eye patch.
21. *coxcomb*] fool.
22–3. *no . . . comedy*] Cf. Shirley who claims he prefers comedy (Prologue,
l. 16).
23. *chaplain*] perhaps a cover for Antonio. See ll. 40–2.
he] i.e. Antonio.
24. *for*] on account of.
the . . . trouble] Jaques reverses the labour of preparation and its reward.
24–5. *to be seen*] to appear; this need mean only that Antonio will appear
responsible, but is perhaps evidence that he has a part in the play (Forker).
See l. 66n.
26. *head*] head-dress of some sort; 'mask' (Walley); 'elaborate hat or wig'
(Forker, who cites Henslowe's inventory of properties as quoted by C. Walter
Hodges, *The Globe Restored*, London, 1953, p. 73). Henslowe lists some substantial properties, such as Argus' three heads, but the present play presumably makes less spectacular demands.
30. *'T wo'*] it would; the joke is about the inadequacy of Rogero's head.
32. *wardrobe*] costume(s).
with ROGERO] Rogero must leave the stage at some point since, as the

2 Servant. Is he gone? In my mind a masque had been fitter for
a marriage.

Jaques. Why, mute? There was no time for't, and the scenes are   35
troublesome.

2 Servant. Half a score deal tacked together in the clouds,
what's that? A throne to come down, and dance; all the
properties have been paid forty times over and are in the
court stock, but the secretary must have a play to show his   40
wit.

Jaques. Did not I tell thee 'twas the chaplain's? Hold your
tongue, mute.

1 Servant. Under the rose, and would this cloth of silver
doublet might never come off again, if there be any more   45
plot than you see in the back of my hand.

2 Servant. You talk of a plot, I'll not give this for the best poet's
plot in the world and if it be not well carried.

Jaques. Well said, mute.

3 Servant. Ha, ha; Pedro since he put on his doublet, has re-   50
peated but three lines, and he has broke five buttons.

---

dialogue indicates, he is '*another Servant*' who enters at l. 56.1.

35. *scenes*] scenery.

37–40. *Half . . . stock*] perhaps an attack on Inigo Jones or a memory of
Jonson's *An Expostulation with Inigo Jones, Wks.*, VIII, 402–6 (Paul Reyher,
Les Masques Anglais, Paris, 1909, p. 381, n. 2). Yet Shirley's description of a
masque in *Love's Cruelty* (II.ii; II, 213) seems to praise three of Jonson's
masques by concentrating on Jones's elaborate staging (Albert Wertheim,
T.N., xxvii, 1972–3, 157–61). See also *The Royal Master*, II.i; IV, 121.

37. *Half . . . together*] ten planks roughly nailed together.

in the clouds] above the stage.

38. *A throne*] a chariot for celestial flights; not a royal throne, which was
usually called a 'state' (Irwin Smith, *Shakespeare's Blackfriars Playhouse*,
London, 1966, p. 424, n. 38).

down . . . dance] awkward punctuation and syntax. 'Throne' may refer also
to its occupant, or we must understand 'and they dance' or 'a throne . . ., and
a dance'. I have tried to indicate this last sense by repunctuating.

39. *paid . . . over*] In the *Expostulation*, Jonson refers to scenery which has
been three times paid for (l. 90). Re-use was a helpful economy.

44. *Under the rose*] just between ourselves.

47. *this*] He makes a gesture.

48. *and if*] if.

carried] carried off, i.e. performed. Note the stress on the co-operative
effort that makes a play.

50–1] presumably there has been comic business with the buttons.

2 Servant. I know not, but by this false beard, and here's hair
    enough to hang a reasonable honest man, I do not remem-
    ber, to say, a strong line indeed in the whole comedy, but
    when the chambermaid kisses the captain.   55

3 Servant. Excellent mute.

Enter ROGERO.

Rogero. They have almost supped, and I cannot find my head
    yet.

Jaques. Play in thine own.

Rogero. Thank you for that, so I may have it made a property; if   60
    I have not a head found me, let master secretary play my
    part himself without it.

Enter ANTONIO.

Antonio. Are you all ready, my masters? The king is coming
    through the gallery; are the women dressed?

1 Servant. Rogero wants a head.   65

Antonio. Here with a pox to you, take mine; you a player? You a
    puppy-dog! Is the music ready?

53–4. remember, to say,] *Gifford;* remember to say *Oct.*   56.1. ROGERO]
Forker; another Servant Oct.

52–4. *but . . . comedy*] Perhaps a 'not' has dropped out after 'here's': ' "if
there's not enough hair (in this beard) to hang an ordinary mortal, I don't
remember saying a single effective line in the play" (with the implication,
"It's obvious that I say many")' (Forker). I prefer Oct.'s reading which con-
tinues the criticism of the play: 'by this false beard, and it's a splendid beard to
swear by, I do not remember, if I may say so, any effective lines in the whole
play'.

54. *to say*] 'I don't remember saying' (Forker); 'if I may say so' (Brooke).
The latter reading (*O.E.D.*, Say, vb., 11) is consistent with 2 Servant playing a
mute.

strong line] vigorous, forceful line. 'Densely or obscurely sententious'
(Forker), as in the fashionable 'strong lines' (see George Williamson, *E.S.*,
xviii, 1936, 152–9). But 2 Servant comments on the lines' power – or lack of
power. Sententiousness seems inappropriate in the action described.

55. *chambermaid*] conventionally lascivious.

60. *it*] his head.

property] stage accessory; perhaps a pun on 'thine own' ('proper') in l. 59
(Forker).

64. *women*] i.e. the boys who play women.

66. *take mine*] evidence that Antonio is an actor in the play (see ll. 24–5).

66–7. *you . . . puppy-dog*] See Introduction, n. 17.

Enter Gentleman-Usher.

Gentleman-Usher. Gentlemen, it is my lady's pleasure that you
 expect till she call for you; there are a company of cavaliers
 in gallant equipage newly alighted, have offered to present   70
 their revels in honour of this hymen; and 'tis her grace's
 command that you be silent till their entertainment be
 over.

1 Servant. Gentlemen!

2 Servant. Affronted!   75

Rogero. Master secretary, there's your head again; a man's a
 man; have I broken my sleep to study fifteen lines for an
 ambassador, and after that a constable, and is it come to
 this?

Antonio. Patience, gentlemen, be not so hot, 'tis but deferred,   80
 and the play may do well enough cold.

Jaques. If it be not presented, the chaplain will have the
 greatest loss, he loses his wits.   *Hautboys* [*within*].

Antonio. This music speaks the king upon entrance; retire,
 retire, and grumble not.   *Exeunt.*   85

Enter KING, CARDINAL, ALVAREZ, DUCHESS, CELINDA,
VALERIA, PLACENTIA, Lords, HERNANDO; *they being set,*
enter COLUMBO, *and five more in rich habits, visarded; be-*
tween every two a torch-bearer; they dance, and after beckon
to Alvarez as desirous to speak with him.

74–5. Gentlemen! / Affronted!] *This ed.;* Gentlemen? / Affronted? *Oct.;*
Gentlemen? / Affronted! *Walley.*

---

70. *equipage*] attire, possibly military.
71. *revels*] masque, entertainment.
76–7. *a . . . man*] A man can stand only so much; proverbial (Tilley, M243).
77. *for*] for the purpose of being.
78. *constable*] court official, especially associated with France.
81. *cold*] i.e. after it has waited for a while. Antonio plays on 'hot'.
83. *loses . . . wits*] (i) runs mad; (ii) loses the praise for the product of his
wits.
83.1. Hautboys] shawms, forerunners of the oboe.
84. *speaks . . . entrance*] announces that the king is about to enter.
85.1. Exeunt] Forker, Like Oct., clears the stage here, thus suggesting a
transition. Gifford and others keep Antonio on stage, but he is in charge of the
servants and is not usually on stage with the Duchess's guests.
85.3. set] seated.
85.4. visarded] masked.

Alvarez. With me!   *They embrace and whisper.*
King. Do you know the masquers, madam?
Duchess.   Not I, sir.
Cardinal. [*Aside*] There's one, but that my nephew is abroad,
    And has more soul than thus to jig upon
    Their hymeneal night, I should suspect   90
    'Twere he.
                            The Masquers *lead in* ALVAREZ.
Duchess. Where's my lord D'Alvarez?   *Recorders* [*within*].
King.   Call in the bridegroom.

    Enter COLUMBO; *four* Masquers *bring in* ALVAREZ *dead, in
    one of their habits, and having laid him down, exeunt.*

Duchess. What mystery is this?
Cardinal.   We want the bridegroom still.
King. Where is Alvarez?
            *Columbo points to the body, they unvisard it, and find
                                Alvarez bleeding.*

Duchess.   Oh, 'tis my lord, he's murdered.
King. Who durst commit this horrid act?
Columbo.   [*Removing his visard*] I, sir.   95
King. Columbo? Ha!
Columbo.   Yes; Columbo that dares stay
    To justify that act.
Hernando.   Most barbarous.
Duchess. Oh my dearest lord!
King. Our guard seize on them all!

---

88. *Aside*] Subst. *Gifford; not in Oct.*   92. *within*] *Gifford; not in Oct.*   92.1.
four Masquers] *Oct.; five Masquers Gifford.*   95. *Removing his visard*] Subst.
Gifford; not in Oct.   99.1] *after* them all! *Forker; after* wedding day? *Oct.;
after* guard *Gifford.*

---

    91. lead in] lead offstage. Gifford and others misread as an entry and omit
the direction as inconsistent with the following s.d. They insert the exit after l.
86.
    92.1 four *Masquers*] One of the original five has been replaced by the dead
Alvarez, dressed in his costume. Gifford assumes 'four' is a mistake for 'five'.
For other criminal masques, see Forsythe, p. 188.
    99. guard] guards. To be of any service to the king they must be ready for a
prompt entrance. Oct. delays their entry. These guards seize Columbo;
others pursue his confederates.

Enter Guard.

                                    This sight doth shake
      All that is man within me; poor Alvarez,   100
      Is this thy wedding day?
Duchess. If you do think there is a heaven, or pains,
      To punish such black crimes i'th' other world,
      Let me have swift and such exemplar justice
      As shall become this great assassinate;   105
      You will take off our faith else, and if here
      Such innocence must bleed and you look on,
      Poor men that call you gods on earth, will doubt
      To obey your laws, nay practise to be devils,
      As fearing if such monstrous sins go on   110
      The saints will not be safe in heaven.
King.   You shall,
      You shall have justice.
Cardinal.   [*Aside*] Now to come off were brave.

                  Enter Servant.

Servant. The masquers, sir, are fled, their horse prepared
      At gate expected to receive 'em, where
      They quickly mounted; coming so like friends,   115
      None could suspect their haste, which is secured
      By advantage of the night.
Columbo. I answer for 'em all, 'tis stake enough
      For many lives, but if that poniard
      Had voice, it would convince they were but all   120

112. *Aside*] Subst. *Gifford; not in Oct.*   115. mounted;] *Forker;* mounted,
Oct.; mounted: *Gifford.*

---

      104. *exemplar*] such as may warn others.
      105. *assassinate*] murder, or murderer.
      106. *take off*] destroy.
      107. *look on*] i.e. without doing anything.
      108. *doubt*] be afraid.
      109. *practise*] plan, endeavour.
      112. *to come off*] i.e. for Columbo to get free.
      brave] excellent.
      113. *horse*] horses.
      115. *mounted; coming*] Oct.'s comma allows 'coming' to refer either to their
reappearance at the gate or to their original arrival.
      116. *secured*] made safe.
      119–20. *poniard . . .voice*] It is bloody.

Spectators of my act; and now if you
Will give your judgements leave, though at the first
Face of this object your cool bloods were frighted,
I can excuse this deed and call it justice,
An act your honours and your office, sir,   125
Is bound to build a law upon, for others
To imitate; I have but took his life,
And punished her with mercy, who had both
Conspired to kill the soul of all my fame.
Read there—[*Gives the Duchess's letter to the King.*] and
   read an injury as deep   130
In my dishonour as the devil knew
A woman had capacity or malice
To execute. Read there how you were cozened, sir,
Your power affronted, and my faith, her smiles
A juggling witchcraft to betray and make   135
My love her horse to stalk withal, and catch
Her curlèd minion.

Cardinal.   Is it possible
The Duchess could dissemble so, and forfeit
Her modesty with you and to us all?
Yet I must pity her; my nephew has   140
Been too severe, though this affront would call
A dying man from prayers, and turn him tiger,
There being nothing dearer than our fame,
Which, if a common man, whose blood has no
Ingredient of honour, labour to   145
Preserve, a soldier, by his nearest tie
To glory, is above all others, bound

---

130. *Gives the Duchess's letter to the King.*] *Gifford; not in Oct.*

123. *object*] sight, spectacle. See *Lr.*, V.iii.238.
125. *act*] act that.
your office] i.e. you as king.
129. *soul . . . fame*] an echo of the Cardinal's words at the end of II.iii.
130–1. *as deep . . . dishonour*] which dishonours me as deeply.
134. *faith*] trust in her, or his own fidelity.
136. *horse to stalk*] i.e. stalking-horse; the Duchess has used her engagement as a cover for pursuing Alvarez.
   137. *minion*] favourite (with strong sexual overtones).
   139. *modesty*] reputation for chaste behaviour.
   146–7. *by . . . glory*] by being bound so very closely to honour. Forker glosses 'his life'.

To vindicate; and yet it might have been
Less bloody.
Hernando.   [*Aside*] Charitable devil!
King. Reads. 'I pray, my lord, release under your hand   150
    what you dare challenge in my love or person, as a just
    forfeit to myself; this act will speak you honourable to my
    thoughts, and when you have conquered thus yourself,
    you may proceed to many victories, and after, with safety
    of your fame, visit again the lost Rosaura.'   155
To this your answer was a free resign?
Columbo. Flattered with great opinion of her faith,
    And my desert of her (with thought that she,
    Who seemed to weep and chide my easy will
    To part with her, could not be guilty of   160
    A treason or apostasy so soon,
    But rather meant this a device to make
    Me expedite the affairs of war), I sent
    That paper, which her wickedness, not justice,
    Applied, what I meant trial, her divorce;   165
    I loved her so, I dare call heaven to witness
    I knew not whether I loved most; while she,
    With him whose crimson penitence I provoked,
    Conspired my everlasting infamy;
    Examine but the circumstance.
Cardinal.   'Tis clear,   170
    This match was made at home before she sent
    That cunning writ in hope to take him off,
    As knowing his impatient soul would scorn

148–9. To ... bloody] *Gifford; one line in Oct.*   149. *Aside*] *Walley; not in*
Oct.   150–55.] *In italics, Oct.*

150–5.] See II.i.128–31n.
151. *challenge*] claim.
151–2. *as . . . myself*] i.e. as her due.
157. *Flattered*] i.e. deceived.
165. *Applied*] 'interpreted as' (Brooke).
divorce] break-up of engagement.
167. *whether*] which of the two, i.e. heaven, or the Duchess.
168. *whose . . . provoked*] whom I compelled to pay for his sin with death.
170. *circumstance*] facts of the case.
171. *This match*] i.e. of Alvarez and the Duchess.
172. *writ*] letter; meaning not recorded after *Spanish Tragedy*, 1592
(*O.E.D.* 1d).
    take . . . off] be rid of him.

To own a blessing came on crutches to him;
It was not well to raise his expectation,—   175
Had you, sir, no affront—to ruin him
With so much scandal and contempt.
King.   We have
    Too plentiful a circumstance to accuse
    You, madam, as the cause of your own sorrows,
    But not without an accessary, more   180
    Than young Alvarez.
Cardinal.   Any other instrument?
King. Yes I am guilty, with herself and Don
    Columbo, though our acts looked several ways,
    That thought a lover might so soon be ransomed;
    And did exceed the office of a king   185
    To exercise dominion over hearts,
    That owe to the prerogative of heaven
    Their choice, or separation; you must therefore,
    When you do kneel for justice and revenge,
    Madam, consider me a lateral agent   190
    In poor Alvarez' tragedy.
1 Lord. It was your love to Don Columbo, sir.
Hernando. [*To 2 Lord*] So, so; the king is charmed; do you
    observe
    How, to acquit Columbo, he would draw

---

176. affront—] *Oct.;* affront? *Gifford.*   184. ransomed;] ransom'd; *uncorr.*
Oct.; ransom'd, *corr. Oct.*   193. *To 2 Lord*] *This ed.; not in Oct.; Aside*
Walley.

---

    174. *own*] accept.
    on crutches] hesitantly, unwillingly. Cf. *Love in a Maze,* V.v; II, 364, and
The Duke's Mistress, V.iv; IV, 272.
    176. *Had . . . affront*] even if it weren't an insult to you. Gifford and other
edd. repunctuate: 'weren't you insulted too?'
    ruin] The root sense, 'fall, cause to fall', from Latin *ruere* is stressed by
'raise' in the previous line.
    177-81. *We . . . Alvarez*] We have more than enough evidence to accuse
you of causing your own sorrows, but others are to blame, too, besides
Alvarez. Note the royal 'we'.
    181. *instrument*] agent.
    183. *our . . . ways*] we had varying purposes.
    184. *ransomed*] 'bought off' (Neilson).
    186. *To exercise*] in exercising.
    190. *lateral agent*] an accessary.
    193. *charmed*] by the Cardinal.

Himself into the plot; heaven, is this justice?   195
Cardinal. Your judgement is divine in this.
King.   And yet,
      Columbo cannot be secure, and we
      Just in his pardon, that durst make so great
      And insolent a breach of law and duty.
2 Lord. [*To Hernando*] Ha, will he turn again?
King.   And should we leave   200
      This guilt of blood to heaven, which cries, and strikes
      With loud appeals the palace of eternity,
      Yet here is more to charge Columbo than
      Alvarez' blood, and bids me punish it,
      Or be no king.
Hernando.   [*To Lords*] 'Tis come about, my lords.   205
King. And if I should forgive
      His timeless death, I cannot the offence,
      That with such boldness struck at me. Has my
      Indulgence to your merits, which are great,
      Made me so cheap, your rage could meet no time   210
      Nor place for your revenge, but where my eyes
      Must be affrighted and affronted with
      The bloody execution? This contempt
      Of majesty transcends my power to pardon,
      And you shall feel my anger, sir.   215
Hernando. [*Aside*] Thou shalt have one short prayer more for
      that.

---

200. *To Hernando*] *This ed.; not in Oct.; Aside Walley.*   205. *To Lords*] *This
ed.; not in Oct.; Aside Walley.*   216. *Aside*] *Walley; not in Oct.*

---

197. *secure*] (i) free from care; (ii) unharmed.
198. *that*] who (Columbo).
201. *which cries*] The antecedent is 'blood'. Cf. Genesis, iv.10.
203–5. *Yet . . . king*] Yet there is more than Alvarez's murder to charge
Columbo with, and it is my duty as king to punish his offences. The repeated
'yet' (ll. 196 and 203) marks the king's veering judgement.
208. *struck at me*] See Introduction, p. 20. See *Bussy D'Ambois*, I.ii.131, for
the avoiding of violence in the king's presence.
210. *meet*] find.
216. *Thou*] Hernando refers familiarly to the king. Respect for superiors
demands the less informal 'you'.

Columbo. Have I i'th' progress of my life
　　No actions to plead me up deserving,
　　Against this ceremony?
Cardinal.　　　　　　　　Contain yourself.
Columbo. I must be dumb then; where is honour?　　　220
　　And gratitude of kings, when they forget
　　Whose hand secured their greatness? Take my head off,
　　Examine then which of your silken lords,
　　As I have done, will throw himself on dangers,
　　Like to a floating island move in blood,　　　225
　　And where your great defence calls him to stand
　　A bulwark, upon his bold breast to take
　　In death, that you may live: but soldiers are
　　Your valiant fools, whom when your own securities
　　Are bleeding you can cherish, but when once　　　230
　　Your state and nerves are knit, not thinking when
　　To use their surgery again, you cast
　　Them off, and let them hang in dusty armouries,
　　Or make it death to ask for pay.
King　　　　　　　　　　No more,

217–19. Have ... ceremony?] *Oct.;* Have I, / I'the ... actions / To plead,
deserving **** me up / Against this ***** ceremony? *Gifford.*

217–9. *Have . . . ceremony?*] 'corrupt and incomplete' (Gifford), but the
meaning is clear: 'have I in the past done nothing which might stand in my
favour against this formal judgement?' Columbo's outburst is to be expected
from a discontented soldier; cf. *The Doubtful Heir*, I.i; IV, 285.
223–8. *Examine . . . death*] Examine which of your lords will throw himself
on dangers, will move in blood, or will take in death. 'To take' may be an error
caused by 'to stand' in the previous line (Forker). Shirley has forgotten his
continuing structure and is now outlining the duty of a soldier, which is 'to
take in death'.
225. *floating island*] Cf. Middleton and Dekker, *Roaring Girl*, I.ii.31: 'like a
floating Iland, seemes to move' (Dekker, *Wks.*, III, 17).
228–33. *but . . . armouries*] The soldier who protects the state is represented as armour to be hung up when not needed. Forker finds the idea of armour
performing surgery grotesque, but the image of healing the state is applied to
the soldiers *before* they are likened to suits of armour.
229–30. *when . . . bleeding*] when the state's safety is threatened.
231. *nerves*] sinews.
　knit] healed.
232. *their*] i.e. the soldiers'.
234. *make . . . pay*] impose the death penalty on those who demand pay;

We thought to have put your victory and merits   235
In balance with Alvarez' death, which while
Our mercy was to judge, had been your safety;
But the affront to us, made greater by
This boldness to upbraid our royal bounty,
Shall tame or make you nothing.

[*1*] *Lord.*   [*To Hernando*] Excellent.   240
Hernando. [*To Lords*] The Cardinal is not pleased.
Cardinal.   [*To Columbo*] Humble yourself
To th' king.

Columbo.   And beg my life? Let cowards do't
That dare not die, I'll rather have no head
Than owe it to his charity.

King. To th' castle with him.   245

                    [*Exeunt* Guard *with* COLUMBO.]
Madam, I leave you to your grief, and what
The king can recompense to your tears, or honour
Of your dead lord, expect.

Duchess.   This shows like justice.

                              Exeunt.

240.[*1*] *Lord.*] *Walley; Lor. Oct.; [2] Lo, Baskervill.   To Hernando*] *This ed.;
not in Oct.; Aside Walley.   241. To Lords*] *This ed.; not in Oct.; Aside
Walley.   To Columbo*] *Forker; not in Oct.   245.1.*] *Subst. Gifford; not in
Oct.*

---

perhaps a reference to the English army of 1641 which was near mutiny
because Charles did not have the means to pay it (Forker).
     237. *had been*] would have been.
     245. *th' castle*] prison. Cf. *The Young Admiral*, II.i; III, 116.

Act IV

Enter two Lords, HERNANDO.

1 Lord. This is the age of wonders.
2 Lord.   Wondrous mischiefs.
Hernando. Among those guards which some call tutelar angels,
    Whose office is to govern provinces,
    Is there not one will undertake Navarre?
    Hath heaven forsook us quite?
1 Lord.   Columbo at large!   5
2 Lord. And graced now more than ever.
1 Lord.   He was not pardoned,
    That word was prejudicial to his fame.
Hernando. But as the murder done had been a dream
    Vanished to memory, he's courted as
    Preserver of his country; with what chains   10
    Of magic does this Cardinal hold the king?
2 Lord. What will you say, my lord, if they enchant
    The Duchess now; and by some impudent art,
    Advance a marriage to Columbo yet?
Hernando. Say? I'll say no woman can be saved, nor is't   15
    Fit, indeed, any should pretend to heaven
    After one such impiety in their sex,
    And yet my faith has been so staggered since

---

5. large!] *Gifford;* large? *Oct.*

---

2. *tutelar*] guardian, appointed to watch over a specific place.
6. *graced*] favoured.
not pardoned] his crime has been forgotten rather than forgiven.
9. *to memory*] from memory.
10–11. *chains | Of magic*] Cf. III.ii.193.
16. *pretend*] aspire.

The king restored Columbo, I'll be now
Of no religion.

1 Lord.   'Tis not possible   20
She can forgive the murder, I observed
Her tears.

Hernando.   Why so did I, my lord,
And if they be not honest, 'tis to be
Half damned to look upon a woman weeping.
When do you think the Cardinal said his prayers?   25

2 Lord. I know not.

Hernando.   Heaven forgive my want of charity,
But if I were to kill him, he should have
No time to pray; his life could be no sacrifice,
Unless his soul went too.

1 Lord.   That were too much.

Hernando. When you mean to dispatch him, you may give   30
Time for confession; they have injured me
After another rate.

2 Lord. You are too passionate, cousin.

        Enter COLUMBO, Colonels, ALPHONSO, Courtiers; *they pass
                over the stage.*

Hernando. How the gay men do flutter to congratulate
His gaol delivery! There's one honest man;   35

19–20. *I'll . . . religion*] I won't believe in anything. Cf. *The Sisters*, I.i; V, 361.

26–9. *Heaven . . . too*] The Cardinal's life will not atone for his crimes; his soul must also be destroyed. Cf. Hamlet's desire to damn Claudius (III.iii.88–95).

29. *too much*] too harsh. The Lords lack Hernando's personal animus.

31. *confession*] possibly an indication that the author was a Roman Catholic, or merely an appropriate reference in a play set in Spain.

they] Columbo and the Cardinal.

32. *After . . . rate*] on a different scale, i.e. one which calls for harsher punishment.

33. *cousin*] term of friendship.

33.1–2. *they . . . stage*] perhaps technical term for an entry through the yard, over the platform, and out by the yard (A. Nicoll, *Sh.S.*, xii, 1959, 47–55). T. J. King disagrees (*Shakespearean Staging, 1599–1642*, Cambridge, Mass., 1971, p. 18).

34. *gay*] (i) showy; (ii) loose, immoral.

35. *There's . . . man*] perhaps a reference to Columbo, whose forthright-ness contrasts with the Cardinal's deceit (Forker). But would an angry

What pity 'tis a gallant fellow should
Depend on knaves for his preferment.
1 Lord. Except this cruelty upon Alvarez,
Columbo has no mighty stain upon him;
But for his uncle—
Hernando.   If I had a son   40
Of twelve years old, that would not fight with him,
And stake his soul against his Cardinal's cap,
I would disinherit him; time has took a lease
But for three lives I hope, a fourth may see
Honesty walk without a crutch.
2 Lord.   This is   45
But air and wildness.
Hernando.   I'll see the Duchess.
[*1 Lord.*] You may do well to comfort her.
We must attend the king.
Hernando.   Your pleasures.

                                   Exit HERNANDO.

                    Enter KING *and* CARDINAL.

1 Lord. [*To 2 Lord*] A man of a brave soul.
2 Lord.   The less his safety;
The king and Cardinal in consult.   50
King. [*To Cardinal*] Commend us to the Duchess, and
     employ

47. *1 Lord.*] *Gifford; line given to Hernando in Oct.*   her.] *Corr. Oct.; her,
uncorr. Oct.*   49. *To 2 Lord*] *Forker; not in Oct.; Aside Baskervill.*   51. *To
Cardinal*] *Forker; not in Oct.*

Hernando praise Columbo as the '*one*' honest man? Even 1 Lord in ll. 38–9
speaks only of 'no mighty stain'. Possibly Hernando means himself and
gestures to that effect; or he comments generally on the world's dishonesty in
words intended to echo *Tim.*, IV.iii.496–7: 'I do proclaim / One honest man –
mistake me not, but one.'

     43–4. *lease . . . lives*] A lease was the length of time – in this case for three
consecutive lives – during which possession of a property was guaranteed
(Stone, pp. 179–80 and 312–13). Once the three lives on whose length the
lease depends are over, then honesty will walk freely again; i.e. if Columbo
and the Cardinal follow Alvarez in death evil times will end.

     47.] All edd. reassign to 1 Lord; possibly Hernando suggests the lords
should follow his example, and they demur, but such a reading seems less
likely. An ambiguously placed s.h. in manuscript could explain the mistake
(Forker).

     49. *A . . . soul*] i.e. Hernando.

What language you think fit and powerful,
To reconcile her to some peace. My lords.
Cardinal. Sir, I possess all for your sacred uses.

Exeunt severally.

ACT IV, SCENE ii

Enter ANTONIO *and* CELINDA.

Antonio. Madam, you are the welcomest lady living.
Celinda. To whom, master secretary?
Antonio.   If you have mercy
    To pardon so much boldness, I durst say
    To me—I am a gentleman.
Celinda.   And handsome.
Antonio. But my lady has much wanted you.   5
Celinda. Why, master secretary?
Antonio. You are the prettiest,—
Celinda. So.
Antonio. The wittiest,—
Celinda. So.   10
Antonio. The merriest lady i'th' court.
Celinda. And I was wished to make the Duchess pleasant.
Antonio. She never had so deep a cause of sorrow;
    Her chamber's but a coffin of a larger
    Volume, wherein she walks so like a ghost,   15
    'Twould make you pale to see her.
Celinda.   Tell her grace
    I attend here.
Antonio.   I shall most willingly.
    [*Aside*] A spirited lady, would I had her in my closet;
    She is excellent company among the lords,

---

52. powerful, /] *Corr. Oct.;* powerful / *uncorr. Oct.*   0.1. ANTONIO] *Gifford;*
Secretary Oct. (throughout scene).   3. much] *Corr. Oct.;* mmch *uncorr.*
Oct.   12. pleasant.] *Oct.;* pleasant? *Gifford.*   16–17. Tell . . . here] *Gifford;*
one line in Oct.   18. Aside] *Walley; not in Oct.*

---

54. *I . . . uses*] a complimentary sentence: 'everything I own is at your
service.'
    sacred] a flattering reference to divine right.
    12. *wished*] wished for; or possibly, 'invited', a rare meaning (*O.E.D.*, 5c).
    pleasant] cheerful.

Sure she has an admirable treble—madam.   *Exit.*   20
Celinda. I do suspect this fellow would be nibbling,
 Like some whose narrow fortunes will not rise
 To wear things when the invention's rare and new,
 But treading on the heel of pride, they hunt
 The fashion when 'tis crippled, like fell tyrants;   25
 I hope I am not old yet, I had the honour
 To be saluted by our Cardinal's nephew
 This morning; there's a man!

Enter ANTONIO.

Antonio.   I have prevailed.
 Sweet madam, use what eloquence you can
 Uper her, and if ever I be useful   30
 To your ladyship's service, your least breath commands
  me.   [*Exit.*]

Enter DUCHESS.

Duchess. Madam, I come to ask you but one question;
 If you were in my state, my state of grief,
 I mean an exile from all happiness
 Of this world, and almost of heaven, for my   35
 Affliction is finding out despair,
 What would you think of Don Columbo—
Celinda.   Madam?
Duchess. Whose bloody hand wrought all this misery?
 Would you not weep as I do? And wish rather
 An everlasting spring of tears to drown   40
 Your sight, than let your eyes be cursed to see

---

28. prevailed.] prevail'd. *corr. Oct.;* prevail'd, *uncorr. Oct.*   31. Exit.]
Gifford; not in Oct.

20. *treble*] possibly a reference to Celinda's skill as a soprano in madrigals at
court (Forker).
 21.] I suspect this fellow would like to take liberties (literally, 'to take little
bites').
 22–5.] like those who cannot afford garments (= women) when their fashion is new (= chaste), but following after 'pride' (= magnificent and sexually
active men, *O.E.D.,* 6; 11), they hunt the fashion (women) when they are
'damaged goods', and behave mercilessly. I hope I am not yet so old (that I
succumb to such men).
 30–1. *if . . . me*] Note Antonio's courtly speech.
 36. *despair*] the sin without hope of redemption.

The murderer again? And glorious?
So careless of his sin, that he is made
Fit for new parricide, even while his soul
Is purpled o'er, and reeks with innocent blood.   45
But do not, do not answer me, I know
You have so great a spirit—which I want,
The horror of his fact surprising all
My faculties—you would not let him live:
But I, poor I, must suffer more, there's not   50
One little star in heaven will look on me,
Unless to choose me out the mark, on whom
It may shoot down some angry influence.

Enter PLACENTIA.

Placentia. Madam, here's Don Columbo says he must
          Speak with your grace.
Duchess.   But he must not, I charge you.   55
                    [*Exit* PLACENTIA.]

None else wait? Is this well done,
To triumph in his tyranny? Speak, madam,
Speak but your conscience.

Enter COLUMBO *and* ANTONIO.

Antonio.   Sir, you must not see her.
Columbo. Not see her! Were she cabled up above
          The search of bullet, or of fire, were she   60
          Within her grave, and that the toughest mine
          That ever nature teemed and groaned withal,

44. parricide] *In italics, Oct.*   55.1.] *Gifford; not in Oct.*

---

     42. *glorious*] (i) proud; (ii) renowned.
     44. *parricide*] murder of anyone whose person is especially sacred; another favourite word.
     48. *fact*] evil deed.
     51-3. *star . . . influence*] Cf. I.ii.220-1.
     56. *None else wait?*] Does it have to be Columbo alone who visits me?
     58. *Speak . . . conscience*] Speak your mind.
     59. *cabled up*] tied up and, by implication, shut away; used in *The Imposture*, I.ii; V, 191, of nuns shut in a convent.
     60. *search*] range.
     62. *teemed . . . withal*] gave birth to.

I would force some way to see her;

[*Exit* ANTONIO.]

do not fear

I come to court you, madam, y'are not worth

The humblest of my kinder thoughts; I come   65

To show the man you have provoked and lost,

And tell you what remains of my revenge.

Live, but never presume again to marry,

I'll kill the next at th'altar, and quench all

The smiling tapers with his blood; if after   70

You dare provoke the priest and heaven so much,

To take another, in thy bed I'll cut him from

Thy warm embrace, and throw his heart to ravens.

Celinda. This will appear an unexampled cruelty.

Columbo. [*To Celinda*] Your pardon, madam, rage, and my

    revenge   75

Not perfect, took away my eyes; you are

A noble lady, this, not worth your eye-beam,

One of so slight a making, and so thin,

An autumn leaf is of too great a value

To play which shall be soonest lost i'th' air;   80

Be pleased to own me by some name; in your

63.1.] *Subst. Baskervill; not in Oct.*   75. *To Celinda*] *Forker; not in Oct.*
81. name; in] *This ed.;* name, in *Oct.*

63.1.] Oct. has no s.d. but has *Enter Secretary* at l. 86.1. Previous edd., apart
from Baskervill, Forker and Lawrence, omit the latter, but it is more likely
that an exit has been mistakenly omitted than an entrance mistakenly
inserted.

65. *humblest*] meanest.

69. *kill . . . altar*] doubly wicked; cf. *Hamlet*, IV.vii.126.

71. *provoke . . . heaven*] 'Provoke' can also mean 'summon' (Forker – 'summon the priest and anger heaven').

72–3. *in . . . embrace*] Cf. Fernando's similar threat in *The Brothers*, V.iii; I,
264.

75–6. *my . . . perfect*] the fact that my revenge is not complete. The syntax
resembles Latin's absolute construction.

77. *this*] i.e. the Duchess.

your eye-beam] a glance from your eye.

78. *thin*] of little worth.

79–80.] a play on the physical sense of 'thin'; by contrast with Rosaura an
autumn leaf is too valuable to gamble with, i.e. in wagering on which of the
two light things (Rosaura or the leaf) will be sooner blown away.

81. *Be . . . name*] Celinda is invited to acknowledge Columbo as a 'servant',
just as he calls her 'mistress'.

Assurance, I despise to be received
There, let her witness that I call you mistress;
Honour me to make these pearls your carkanet.

[*Gives her a necklace.*]

Celinda. My lord, you are too humble in your thoughts.   85
Columbo. There's no vexation too great to punish her.   *Exit.*

Enter ANTONIO.

Antonio. Now, madam?
Celinda. Away, you saucy fellow; madam, I
    Must be excused if I do think more honourably
    Than you have cause of this great lord.
Duchess.   Why, is not   90
    All womankind concerned to hate what's impious?
Celinda. For my part—
Duchess.   Antonio, is this a woman?
Antonio. I know not whether she be man or woman;
    I should be nimble to find out the experiment,
    She looked with less state when Columbo came.   95
Duchess. [*To Celinda*] Let me entreat your absence. [*Aside*] I
    am cozened in her—
    [*To her*] I took you for a modest, honest lady.
Celinda. Madam, I scorn any accuser, and
    Deducting the great title of a duchess,
    I shall not need one grain of your dear honour   100

82. Assurance, I] *Oct.;* Assurance; I
Walley.   83–4. There . . . carkanet.] *Gifford;* There . . . call / You . . . Pearls /
Your carkanet. *Oct.*   84. *Gives her a necklace.*] *Gifford;* not in *Oct.*   86. *No
s.d.*] *Oct.; Aside Gifford.*   86.1.] *Subst. Oct.; Gifford excises.*   96. *To
Celinda*] *Forker;* not in *Oct.   Aside*] *Subst. Gifford;* not in *Oct.*

81–3. *in . . . There*] to assure you that I despise the Duchess. Oct. leaves it
unclear whether 'in your / Assurance' belongs with the preceding or following
clause. Walley's punctuation suggests, 'as a mark of trust, call me by some
familiar name'.
84. *carkanet*] necklace.
85. *too humble*] i.e. in thinking of me.
86.1.] See note on l. 63.1
94. *find . . . experiment*] test her.
95. *looked . . . state*] behaved with fewer airs.
97. *honest*] respectable.
100. *dear*] precious, with hint of irony.

To make me full weight; if your grace be jealous
I can remove.　　　　　　　　　　　*Exit.*
Antonio.　　　　　She is gone.
Duchess.　　　　　　　　Prithee remove
My fears of her return—

　　　　　　　　　　　Exit ANTONIO.

　　　　　　　　　　she is not worth
Considering, my anger's mounted higher;
He need not put in caution for my next　　　　105
Marriage; Alvarez, I must come to thee,
Thy virgin, wife, and widow, but not till
I ha' paid those tragic duties to thy hearse,
Become my piety and love. But how?
Who shall instruct a way?

　　　　　　　Enter PLACENTIA.

Placentia.　　　　　Madam, Don　　　　110
Hernando much desires to speak with you.
Duchess. Will not thy own discretion think I am
Unfit for visit?
Placentia.　　　　Please your grace, he brings
Something he says imports your ear and love
Of the dead lord Alvarez.
Duchess.　　　　　Then admit him.　　　　115
　　　　　　　　　[*Exit* PLACENTIA.]

　　　Enter [PLACENTIA *with*] HERNANDO.

103.1.] *After* worth *in Oct.*　　107. virgin, wife,] *Oct.;* virgin wife,
Gifford.　　115.1.] *Gifford; not in Oct.*　　115.2. PLACENTIA *with*] *Gifford; not
in Oct.*

---

101. *To . . . weight*] a reference to the legal requirement on tradesmen to
weigh out the full amount. Celinda thinks she is worth as much as the
Duchess.

102. *remove*] (i) go away; (ii) take away. The repetition is probably
unintentional.

102–3. *remove . . . return*] prevent her from coming back.

105–6. *put . . . Marriage*] warn me against marrying again.

109. *Become*] which become.

110–11. *Who . . . Hernando*] The Duchess's question is answered by
Hernando's arrival.

114. *imports*] concerns.

Hernando. I would speak, madam, to yourself.
Duchess.   Your absence.
          [*Exit* PLACENTIA.]

Hernando. I know not how your grace will censure so
          Much boldness, when you know the affairs I come for.
Duchess. My servant has prepared me to receive it,
          If it concern my dead lord.
Hernando.   Can you name   120
          So much of your Alvarez in a breath
          Without one word of your revenge? O madam,
          I come to chide you, and repent my great
          Opinion of your virtue, that can walk,
          And spend so many hours in naked solitude,   125
          As if you thought that no arrears were due
          To his death, when you had paid his funeral charges,
          Made your eyes red, and wept a handkercher;
          I come to tell you that I saw him bleed;
          I, that can challenge nothing in his name   130
          And honour, saw his murdered body warm
          And panting with the labour of his spirits,
          Till my amazed soul shrunk and hid itself,
          While barbarous Columbo grinning stood,
          And mocked the weeping wounds; it is too much   135
          That you should keep your heart alive, so long
          After this spectacle, and not revenge it.
Duchess. You do not know the business of my heart,
          That censure me so rashly; yet I thank you,

116.1.] *Gifford; not in Oct.*   117. your] *Gifford;* you *Oct.*

117. *censure*] judge of.
120–1. *Can . . . breath*] Can you mention Alvarez's death?
123. *to chide*] Cf. *Ham.*, III.iv.110–11, where the ghost chides Hamlet for delay.
125. *naked*] mere.
126. *no . . . due*] nothing else was owed to him.
128. *wept a handkercher*] wept into a handkerchief; or, wept enough to soak a handkerchief.
130. *can challenge nothing*] 'have no claim upon' (Walley).
132. *labour . . . spirits*] 'labor pains of yielding up the ghost' (Forker).
135. *weeping*] i.e. exuding blood.
136. *keep . . . alive*] simply 'stay alive' or, 'keep your emotions alive'.

And if you be Alvarez' friend, dare tell   140
Your confidence that I despise my life,
But know not how to use it in a service,
To speak me his revenger; this will need
No other proof than that to you, who may
Be sent with cunning to betray me, I   145
Have made this bold confession; I so much
Desire to sacrifice to that hovering ghost,
Columbo's life, that I am not ambitious
To keep my own two minutes after it.
Hernando. If you will call me coward, which is equal   150
To think I am a traitor, I forgive it
For this brave resolution, which time
And all the destinies must aid; I beg
That I may kiss your hand for this, and may
The soul of angry honour guide it.
Duchess.   Whither?   155
Hernando. To Don Columbo's heart.
Duchess. It is too weak I fear alone.
Hernando. Alone? Are you in earnest? Why, will it not
Be a dishonour to your justice, madam,
Another arm should interpose? But that   160
It were a saucy act to mingle with you,
I durst, nay I am bound, in the revenge
Of him that's dead—since the whole world has interest
In every good man's loss—to offer it;
Dare you command me, madam?
Duchess.   Not command,   165
But I should more than honour such a truth
In man, that durst against so mighty odds
Appear Alvarez' friend and mine; the Cardinal—
Hernando. Is for the second course, Columbo must

---

147. sacrifice] *Uncorr. Oct.;* sacrifise *corr. Oct.*   158. Why, will] *Gifford;* why? will *Oct.*   164. good man's] *Gifford;* goodmans *Oct.*

140–1. *dare . . . confidence*] probably 'I dare tell you in confidence', although 'dare' could be imperative ('know confidentially', Forker).

147. *hovering*] Cf. Don Andrea in *Spanish Tragedy*, and Hamlet's father (III.iv.103: 'hover o'er me'), who cannot rest until they are avenged.

161. *saucy*] presumptuous.

mingle with] join with.

164. *it*] i.e. 'to mingle with you'.

169. *second course*] of a meal. The Cardinal can be killed later.

Be first cut up, his ghost must lead the dance.   170
   Let him die first.
Duchess. But how?
Hernando. How? With a sword, and if I undertake it,
   I wo' not lose so much of my own honour,
   To kill him basely.
Duchess.   How shall I reward   175
   This infinite service? 'Tis not modesty,
   While now my husband groans beneath his tomb,
   And calls me to his marble bed, to promise
   What this great act might well deserve, myself,
   If you survive the victor, but if thus   180
   Alvarez' ashes be appeased, it must
   Deserve an honourable memory;
   And though Columbo, as he had all power,
   And grasped the fates, has vowed to kill the man
   That shall succeed Alvarez—   185
Hernando. Tyranny!
Duchess.   Yet if ever
   I entertain a thought of love hereafter,
   Hernando from the world shall challenge it,
   Till when, my prayers and fortune shall wait on you.
Hernando. This is too mighty recompense.
Duchess.   'Tis all just.   190
Hernando. If I outlive Columbo I must not
   Expect security at home.
Duchess.   Thou canst
   Not fly where all my fortunes and my love
   Shall not attend to guard thee.

---

170. *lead the dance*] an allusion to the mediaeval concept of the Dance of Death. All degrees of the living were shown dancing with the dead towards the grave.

175. *basely*] in an underhand way. Hernando plans an honourable duel.

179. *myself*] Cf. Bel-Imperia's love for Horatio (*Spanish Tragedy*). Hippolita in *'Tis Pity* promises marriage to Vasques if he will help her take vengeance on Soranzo (II.ii.144–5).

183–4. *as . . . fates*] as if he controlled destiny. Cf. *The Witty Fair One*, III.iii; I, 314: 'I hold my destiny betwixt two fingers'; also *1 Tamburlaine*, I.ii.173, and *'Tis Pity*, V.v.11–12.

185–6.] Hernando's 'Tyranny!' interrupts a complete verse line spoken by the Duchess.

188.] Hernando has first claim on my love. Cf.I.ii.35.
from] picked out from.

Hernando.   If I die—
Duchess. Thy memory   195
    Shall have a shrine, the next within my heart
    To my Alvarez.
Hernando.   Once again your hand;
    Your cause is so religious you need
    Not strengthen it with your prayers, trust it to me.

            Enter PLACENTIA *and* CARDINAL.

Placentia. Madam, the Cardinal.   [*Exit.*]
Duchess.   [*To Hernando*] Will you appear?   200
Hernando. And he had all the horror of the devil
    In's face, I would not balk him.
            He stares upon the Cardinal in his exit.

Cardinal. [*Aside*] What makes Hernando here? I do not like
    They should consult, I'll take no note; [*To Duchess*] the
        king
    Fairly salutes your grace, by whose command   205
    I am to tell you, though his will and actions
    Illimited, stoop not to satisfy
    The vulgar inquisition, he is
    Yet willing to retain a just opinion
    With those that are placed near him; and although   210

198–9. need / Not] *Oct.;* need not / *all modern edd.*   200. *Exit.*] *Forker; not in
Oct.   To Hernando*] *Forker; not in Oct.*   203. *Aside*] *Subst. Gifford; not in
Oct.*

---

198. *religious*] sacred.
199.1.] Again the Cardinal hangs back, as if spying in the background.
201. *And*] if.
202. *balk*] avoid.
202.1.] Cf. *H8*, I.i.114.3–6; 'The Cardinal in his passage fixeth his eye on
Buckingham, and Buckingham on him, both full of disdain.'
203. *What . . . here?*] What is Hernando doing here?
207. *Illimited*] not subject to restraints; a reference to the divine right of
kings.
208. *vulgar inquisition*] i.e. anybody's and everybody's questions.
209. *retain . . . opinion*] 'keep his reputation for being just' (Forker) or,
more generally, 'remain well thought of'.
210–11. *although . . . anger*] Although you look at yourself without the
artificial aid of telescope or magnifying glass, you exaggerate what seems, to
your limited judgement, an injury (since we always see our own wrongs
largest); yet more rational and thoughtful observation would show you that

You look with nature's eye upon yourself,
Which needs no perspective to reach, nor art
Of any optic to make greater, what
Your narrow sense applies an injury,—
Ourselves still nearest to ourselves—but there's   215
Another eye that looks abroad and walks
In search of reason and the weight of things,
With which if you look on him, you will find
His pardon to Columbo cannot be
So much against his justice, as your erring   220
Faith would persuade your anger.

Duchess.   Good, my lord,
Your phrase has too much landscape and I cannot
Distinguish, at this distance you present,
The figure perfect, but indeed my eyes
May pray your lordship find excuse, for tears   225
Have almost made them blind.

Cardinal.   Fair, peace restore 'em!

---

222. cannot /] *Uncorr. Oct.;* cannot, / *corr. Oct.*   223. Distinguish, at this distance you present,] *Gifford;* Distinguish at this distance you present / *uncorr. Oct.;* Distinguish at this distance; you present / *corr. Oct.*   226. Fair, peace] *Oct.;* Fair peace *Gifford.*

---

the king's pardon of Columbo is not as unjust as you think. The Cardinal's winding syntax is blurred by the substitution of 'but' for 'yet' in l. 215; his speech is 'as tortuous and serpentine in construction as it is sophistical in thought' (Forker).

213. *optic*] magnifying glass.

216. *Another eye*] a more objective gaze.

221. *Faith*] belief.

222–6. *Your . . . blind*] Your words are displayed in a far-off prospect and I cannot perfectly distinguish, at the distance at which you present it to me, your central meaning. The Duchess then blames her imperfect vision on her tears. Cf. Forker's gloss on corr. Oct.: 'your speech is all distance to me, and from where I stand I can't make out the details. Expert though you are in rhetorical subtlety, I have difficulty in seeing your meaning (and your body) since my eyes are almost blinded by tears.' For 'landscape' (= 'background in figure painting', 'distant prospect') and 'figure' (= 'representation of human form', 'rhetorical figure', 'human body') see D. S. Bland, *R.E.S.*, N.S., iv(1953), 358–9. I prefer uncorr. Oct. Although the miscorrection 'cannot' need not be evidence of a further miscorrection – 'distance;' – we can have no confidence in the semi-colon's authority. Also uncorr. Oct.'s punctuation makes slightly better sense. L. 227 indicates that the figure *was* presented at a distance. The image is common in Shirley; cf. *Love in a Maze*, II.ii; II, 299.

To bring the object nearer, the king says
He could not be severe to Don Columbo
Without injustice to his other merits,
Which call more loud for their reward and honour,   230
Than you for your revenge; the kingdom made
Happy by those, you only by the last
Unfortunate; nor was it rational,
I speak the king's own language, he should die
For taking one man's breath, without whose valour   235
None now had been alive without dishonour.

Duchess. In my poor understanding, 'tis the crown
 Of virtue to proceed in its own tract,
 Not deviate from honour; if you acquit
 A man of murder 'cause he has done brave   240
 Things in the war, you will bring down his valour
 To a crime, nay to a bawd, if it secure
 A rape, and but teach those that deserve well
 To sin with greater licence; but dispute
 Is now too late, my lord, 'tis done, and you,   245
 By the good king, in tender of my sorrows,
 Sent to persuade me 'tis unreasonable
 That justice should repair me.

Cardinal.   You mistake,

233. Unfortunate;] Uunfortunate; *corr. Oct.;* Uunfortunate, *uncorr.*
Oct.   236. alive without] *Gifford;* alive, without *Oct.*   247. persuade me
'tis] perswade *corr. Oct.;* perswade me, 'tis *uncorr. Oct.*

---

227. *To . . . nearer*] to bring the image closer to your eyes, i.e. to speak more
clearly.
 231. *made*] being made.
 232. *those*] Columbo's merits.
 the last] i.e. thwarted revenge.
 234. *I . . . language*] I quote the king's own words.
 235. *whose*] i.e. Columbo's.
 236.] None would now be alive without the dishonour of being conquered.
Oct.'s comma might just imply that the dishonour would belong to the king
who orders his death.
 238. *tract*] track, pathway.
 239–43. *if . . . rape*] If his valour covers up his wrongdoing you turn that
valour itself into a crime, indeed to rape. 'Rape' = 'violent seizure' (of
Alvarez), but the image of the bawd points to the sexual sense, which is
irrelevant to Columbo and does not here seem to look forward to the
Cardinal's attempted rape.
 246. *tender of*] concern for.
 248. *repair me*] make reparation.

For if Columbo's death could make Alvarez
Live, the king had given him up to law   250
Your bleeding sacrifice; but when his life
Was but another treasure thrown away
To obey a clamorous statute, it was wisdom
To himself and common safety to take off
This killing edge of law, and keep Columbo   255
To recompense the crime by noble acts
And sorrow, that in time might draw your pity.
Duchess. This is a greater tyranny than that
Columbo exercised; he killed my lord,
And you not have the charity to let   260
Me think it worth a punishment.
Cardinal.   To that,
In my own name I answer; I condemn
And urge the bloody guilt against my nephew;
'Twas violent and cruel, a black deed,
A deed whose memory doth make me shudder,   265
An act that did betray a tyrannous nature,
Which he took up in war, the school of vengeance;
And though the king's compassion spare him here,
Unless his heart weep itself out in penitent tears,
Hereafter—   270
Duchess. This sounds
As you were now a good man.
Cardinal.   Does your grace
Think I have conscience to allow the murder?
Although when it was done I did obey
The stream of nature, as he was my kinsman,   275
To plead he might not pay his forfeit life,
Could I do less for one so near my blood?
Consider, Madam, and be charitable,

---

261. punishment.] *Corr. Oct.;* punishment, *uncorr. Oct.*   263. bloody] *Corr.*
Oct.; blody *uncorr. Oct.*   269–70. tears, / Hereafter—] *Corr. Oct.;* tears. /
uncorr. Oct.; tears, hereafter—*Brooke.*

---

253. *clamorous*] 'crying out for punishment' (Forker).
254. *take off*] remove so as to relieve someone.
256. *recompense*] atone for.
262. *In my own name*] He is no longer speaking for the king.
267. *took up*] acquired.
273. *allow*] sanction, approve of.
275. *stream of nature*] blood, kinship.

Let not this wild injustice make me lose
The character I bear, and reverend habit.   280
To make you full acquainted with my innocence,
I challenge here my soul and heaven to witness:
If I had any thought or knowledge with
My nephew's plot or person, when he came
Under the smooth pretence of friend to violate   285
Your hospitable laws, and do that act
Whose frequent mention draws this tear, a whirlwind
Snatch me to endless flames.

Duchess.   I must believe,
And ask your grace's pardon; I confess
I ha' not loved you since Alvarez' death,   290
Though we were reconciled.

Cardinal.   I do not blame
Your jealousy, nor any zeal you had
To prosecute revenge against me, madam,
As I then stood suspected, nor can yet
Implore your mercy to Columbo; all   295
I have to say is to retain my first
Opinion and credit with your grace,
Which you may think I urge not out of fear
Or ends upon you,—since, I thank the king,

---

282. witness: /] *Forker; witness | Oct.; witness, Gifford.*

---

279. *wild injustice*] Cf. Bacon's definition of revenge as 'a kind of wild justice' ('Of Revenge', *Essays*).

279–80. *lose . . . habit*] 'forfeit in your eyes the character which my priestly garb symbolizes' (Forker).

282–8. *I . . . flames*] Oct. forces us to read, 'I challenge . . . to witness / If . . .'. At the end of the speech we realise the Cardinal has said, 'if I had . . . a whirlwind snatch me'. The loose construction is plausible as a mark of realistic speech, but to aid the reader I have indicated the main division by repunctuating.

282. *challenge*] summon.

283. *with*] of.

284. *person*] an allusion to Columbo's disguise. III.ii.88–91 indicates at least a thought.

287. *whirlwind*] a common image which Shirley uses repeatedly, often with 'snatch', e.g. *The Court Secret*, III.ii; V, 474. See also Dekker and Massinger, *The Virgin Martyr*, IV.iii.119 (Dekker, *Wks.*, III,446).

292. *jealousy*] distrust.

296–7. *my first | Opinion*] what you originally thought of me.

299. *ends*] ulterior motives.

I stand firm on the base of royal favour—   300
But for your own sake, and to show I have
Compassion of your sufferings.
Duchess.   You have cleared
A doubt, my lord, and by this fair remonstrance
Given my sorrow so much truce to think
That we may meet again, and yet be friends.   305
But be not angry, if I still remember
By whom Alvarez died, and weep, and wake
Another justice with my prayers.
Cardinal.   All thoughts
That may advance a better peace, dwell with you.   *Exit*.
Duchess. How would this cozening statesman bribe my faith   310
With flatteries to think him innocent!
No, if his nephew die, this Cardinal must not
Be long-lived; all the prayers of a wronged widow
Make firm Hernando's sword, and my own hand
Shall have some glory in the next revenge;   315
I will pretend my brain with grief distracted;
It may gain easy credit, and beside
The taking off examination
For great Columbo's death, it makes what act
I do, in that believed want of my reason,   320
Appear no crime, but my defence; look down,
Soul of my lord, from thy eternal shade,
And unto all thy blest companions boast
Thy Duchess busy to revenge thy ghost.   *Exit*.

---

320. do, in that] *Baskervill;* do in that *Oct*.

---

308. *Another justice*] i.e. God's. Several times the gap between earthly and
heavenly affairs is stressed by 'other' and 'another'.

316. *I will pretend*] Rosaura's madness is an expected ingredient in a
revenge play.

318.] preventing an enquiry about.

320. *believed*] supposed.

321. *Appear . . . defence*] Any crime that I commit will be evidence that I
am deranged and will thus protect me.

322. *eternal shade*] a combination of Christian and classical ideas of the
afterlife (Forker).

ACT IV, Scene iii

Enter COLUMBO, HERNANDO, ALPHONSO, Colonel.

Columbo. Hernando, now I love thee, and do half
    Repent the affront my passion threw upon thee.
Hernando. You wo' not be too prodigal o' your penitence.
Columbo. This makes good thy nobility of birth,
    Thou mayst be worth my anger and my sword,   5
    If thou dost execute as daringly
    As thou provok'st a quarrel; I did think
    Thy soul a starveling or asleep.
Hernando.   You'll find it
    Active enough to keep your spirit waking,
    Which to exasperate, for yet I think   10
    It is not high enough to meet my rage—
    D'ye smile?
Columbo.   This noise is worth it; gentlemen,
    I'm sorry this great soldier has engaged
    Your travail, all his business is to talk.
Hernando. A little of your lordship's patience;   15
    You shall have other sport, and swords that will
    Be as nimble 'bout your heart as you can wish;
    'Tis pity more than our two single lives
    Should be at stake.
Colonel.   Make that no scruple, sir.

12. D'ye] *Brooke;* D'ee *Oct.*   it; gentlemen,] *Subst. Gifford;* it, Gentlemen;
Oct.   14. travail] *Gifford;* travel *Oct.*

    0.1.] Since Columbo's opening words imply delight at Hernando's keeping
faith, we can assume with Gifford that Columbo and Alphonso enter from one
side, Hernando and his second from the other.
    1. *thee*] Although later in the scene the distinctions between 'thou' and 'you'
seem blurred, Columbo's 'thee' in his opening speeches sounds deliberately
patronising. Hernando addresses Columbo as 'you'.
    3. *too prodigal*] an ironic comment on 'half / Repent'.
    4. *makes good*] confirms.
    9. *spirit*] temper; with a play on 'soul' (l. 8).
    11. *high enough*] angry enough.
    12. *noise*] mere sound.
    14. *travail*] trouble. 'Travel' (Oct.) could mean either 'a journey' or
'travail'. The latter meaning seems more likely here. To avoid misleading the
modern reader I have altered what, at first sight, seems an acceptable modern
spelling.
    18–19. *'Tis . . . stake*] It was sometimes the custom for seconds to fight

Hernando. To him then that survives, if fate allow   20
    That difference, I speak that he may tell
    The world I came not hither on slight anger,
    But to revenge my honour, stained and trampled on
    By this proud man; when general, he commanded
    My absence from the field.
Columbo.   I do remember,   25
    And I'll give your soul now a discharge.
Hernando.   I come
    To meet it, if your courage be so fortunate.
    But there is more than my own injury
    You must account for, sir, if my sword prosper,
    Whose point and every edge is made more keen   30
    With young Alvarez' blood, in which I had
    A noble interest; does not that sin benumb
    Thy arteries, and turn the guilty flowings
    To trembling jelly in thy veins? Canst hear
    Me name that murder, and thy spirits not   35
    Struck into air, as thou wert shot by some
    Engine from heaven?
Columbo.   You are the Duchess' champion;
    Thou hast given me a quarrel now; I grieve
    It is determined all must fight, and I
    Shall lose much honour in his fall.
Hernando.   That Duchess,   40

26–7. I . . . fortunate] *Gifford; one line in Oct.*

---

alongside the principals. See Sir William Segar, *The Booke of Honor and Armes* (1590), p. 1; also Bowers, *J.E.G.P.*, xxxvi, 1937, 40–65.

26. *your*] Columbo grows angry and abandons the merely contemptuous 'thou'.

soul . . . discharge] Having dismissed Hernando from the army, Columbo will now release his soul from his body.

27. *if . . . fortunate*] if you are lucky enough to kill me.

31. *With . . . blood*] The desire for personal revenge is whetted by the need to avenge Alvarez's death.

33–4. *turn . . . jelly*] Cf. *Wint.*, I.ii.417–18: 'my best blood turn / To an infected jelly'; also *The Wedding*, IV.iv; I, 428.

33. *flowings*] i.e. blood. 'Guilty flowings' echoes *The Royal Master*, IV.i; IV, 156.

35–6. *not | Struck*] not be struck.

37. *Engine*] weapon such as a military catapult.

38–40. *I . . . fall*] Columbo regrets that the seconds must also fight. His reference to 'his fall' may be addressed to one or both seconds, or he may with

　　Whom but to mention with thy breath is sacrilege,
　　An orphan of thy making, and condemned
　　By thee to eternal solitude, I come
　　To vindicate, and while I am killing thee,
　　By virtue of her prayers sent up for justice,　　　　45
　　At the same time in heaven I am pardoned for't.
Columbo. I cannot hear the bravo.
Hernando.　　　　　　　　　　Two words more
　　And take your chance; before you all I must
　　Pronounce that noble lady without knowledge
　　Or thought of what I undertake for her.　　　　50
　　Poor soul, she's now at her devotions,
　　Busy with heaven, and wearing out the earth
　　With her stiff knees, and bribing her good angel
　　With treasures of her eyes, to tell her lord
　　How much she longs to see him; my attempt　　　　55
　　Needs no commisssion from her; were I
　　A stranger in Navarre, the inborn right
　　Of every gentleman to Alvarez' loss
　　Is reason to engage their swords and lives
　　Against the common enemy of virtue.　　　　60
Columbo. Now have you finished? I have an instrument
　　Shall cure this noise, and fly up to thy tongue
　　To murder all thy words.
Hernando.　　　　　　　　　One little knot
　　Of phlegm that clogs my stomach, and I ha' done;

---

deliberate rudeness speak of Hernando in the third instead of the second person.

　42. *orphan*] one bereft of happiness; a rare meaning.

　47. *bravo*] Perhaps Columbo means 'bravado' as in Jonson's *Silent Woman*, III.vi.109 (Forker), but he may be continuing his pretence of ignoring Hernando ('his fall'): 'I cannot (bear to) hear the villain'.

　48–50. *before . . . her*] Hernando's proclamation seems unlikely to deceive, although his desire to protect the Duchess is understandable.

　53. *good angel*] Cf. Navarre's earlier need of a 'tutelar angel' (IV.i.2).

　54. *treasures*] tears, often compared to jewels.

　58. *to Alvarez' loss*] to revenge the murder of Alvarez.

　60. *common . . . virtue*] As in 'the common enemy of man' (*Mac.*, III.i.68) this suggests the devil.

　63–4. *One . . . stomach*] The image is of clearing the throat ('stomach'). Speech is appropriately 'phlegm', the cold fluid, in contrast to the heat of combat. Also Hernando metaphorically spits at Columbo. Cf. Herbert, *The Church Porch*, where England is adjured to 'Spit out thy flegme' (l. 92).

You have an uncle called a Cardinal;   65
Would he were lurking now about thy heart,
That the same wounds might reach you both, and send
Your reeling souls together. Now have at you.

Alphonso. [*To Colonel*] We must not, sir, be idle.

> *They fight; Columbo's second [Alphonso] slain.*

Hernando. What think you now of praying?

Columbo.   Time enough;   70

> *He kills Hernando's second [the Colonel].*

Commend me to my friend; the scales are even;
I would be merciful, and give you time
Now to consider of the other world,
You'll find your soul benighted presently.

Hernando. I'll find my way i'th' dark.

> *They fight, and close; Columbo gets both the*
> *swords, and Hernando takes up the second's weapon.*

Columbo.   A stumble's dangerous.   75
Now ask thy life—ha?

Hernando.   I despise to wear it
A gift from any but the first bestower.

Columbo. I scorn a base advantage—

> *Columbo throws away one of the swords.*
> *They fight; Hernando wounds Columbo.*

                                        ha!

Hernando.   I am now
Out of your debt.

Columbo.   Th'hast done't, and I forgive thee.
Give me thy hand, when shall we meet again?   80

---

69. *To Colonel*] *Forker; not in Oct.*   69.1. *Alphonso*] *Gifford; not in Oct.*   79. Th'hast done't] *Subst. Gifford;* Th'ast don't *Oct.*

---

68. *reeling*] unsteady; not firm in virtue and thus liable to 'reel to death' (see II.i.43).

71. *Commend . . . friend*] an ironic compliment, inviting the colonel to bear greetings to Alphonso.

the . . . even] one is dead on each side.

75. *stumble*] an evil omen; Tilley, T259.

78.1. throws . . . swords] See the earlier comments on Columbo's relative nobility (IV.i.38–9). He gives up his advantage.

80. *Give . . . hand*] Hernando's reply indicates that he refuses the offered reconciliation.

Hernando. Never, I hope.

Columbo. I feel life ebb apace, yet I'll look upwards,
And show my face to heaven.   [*Dies.*]

Hernando.   The matter's done,
I must not stay to bury him.   *Exit.*

---

83. *Dies.*] *Gifford; not in Oct.*

81–4.] could be relined; . . . apace, / . . . heaven. / . . . him.
82. *look upwards*] Cf. *Bussy D'Ambois*, V.iii.135–6: 'I'll not complain to earth yet, but to heaven, / And (like a man) look upwards even in death.'

Act V

ACT V, Scene i

Enter two Lords.

1 Lord. Columbo's death doth much afflict the king.
2 Lord. I thought the Cardinal would have lost his wits
    At first, for's nephew, it drowns all the talk
    Of the other that were slain.
1 Lord.   We are friends.
    I do suspect Hernando had some interest   5
    And knew how their wounds came.
2 Lord.   His flight confirms it,
    For whom the Cardinal has spread his nets.
1 Lord. He is not so weak to trust himself at home
    To his enemy's grip.
2 Lord.   All strikes not me so much
    As that the Duchess, most oppressèd lady,
    Should be distracted, and before Columbo   10
    Was slain.
1 Lord.   But that the Cardinal should be made
    Her guardian is to me above that wonder.
2 Lord. So it pleased the king, and she, with that small stock
    Of reason left her, is so kind and smooth   15
    Upon him.
1 Lord.   She's turned a child again; a madness
    That would ha' made her brain and blood boil high,

---

4. *the other*] Alphonso and the colonel.
We . . . friends] They can therefore speak in confidence.
7. *spread . . . nets*] Cf. V.ii.110–13 where Antonio imagines the Cardinal himself caught in a net.
9. *All strikes not me*] None of this strikes me.
11. *distracted*] deranged.
13. *wonder*] Cf. II.iii.59 and 80, III.i.6 and IV.i.1.

    In which distemper she might ha' wrought something—
2 Lord. Had been to purpose.
1 Lord. The Cardinal is cunning, and howe'er   20
    His brow does smile, he does suspect Hernando
    Took fire from her, and waits a time to punish it.
2 Lord. But what a subject of disgrace and mirth
    Hath poor Celinda made herself by pride,
    In her belief Columbo was her servant.   25
    Her head hath stooped much since he died, and she
    Almost ridiculous at court.

       Enter CARDINAL, ANTONELLI, Servant.

1 Lord.   The Cardinal
    Is come into the garden, now—
Cardinal.   Walk off.
       [*Exeunt* Lords. *Antonelli and Servant move aside.*]

    It troubles me the Duchess by her loss
    Of brain is now beneath my great revenge;   30
    She is not capable to feel my anger,
    Which like to unregarded thunder spent
    In woods, and lightning aimed at senseless trees,
    Must idly fall, and hurt her not, not to
    That sense her guilt deserves; a fatal stroke,   35
    Without the knowledge for what crime, to fright her
    When she takes leave, and make her tug with death

28.1.] *This ed.; not in Oct.; Exeunt Lords. Gifford.*   36. crime, to] *Gifford;* crime to *Oct.*

    19.] would have achieved something. The Duchess has successfully deceived those around her.
    29–46.] This soliloquy of villainous self-revelation has many predecessors. Forsythe (p. 160) includes Richard III, Iago, Edmund and Volpone, as well as Shirley's own villains.
    30. *beneath . . . revenge*] not worth taking revenge on since she will not suffer enough.
    31. *to feel*] of feeling.
    33. *senseless*] incapable of feeling.
    35. *sense*] intensity of pain.
    36. *Without . . . crime*] without her knowing what she has been punished for.
    36–7. *to fright . . . make*] to fright and to make.
    37. *tug with death*] another favourite image. Cf. *The Wedding*, IV.iv; I, 428. In *2H6*, III.ii.173, Duke Humphrey tugs 'for life'.

Until her soul sweat, is a pigeon's torment,
And she is sent a babe to the other world;
Columbo's death will not be satisfied,   40
And I but wound her with a two-edged feather;
I must do more, I have all opportunity,
She by the king now made my charge, but she's
So much a turtle I shall lose by killing her,
Perhaps do her a pleasure and preferment;   45
That must not be.

        Enter CELINDA *with a parchment.*

Antonelli. Is not this she that would be thought to have been
  Columbo's mistress? Madam, his grace is private,
  And would not be disturbed; you may displease him.
Celinda. What will your worship wager that he shall   50
  Be pleased again before we part?
Antonelli. I'll lay this diamond, madam, 'gainst a kiss,
  And trust yourself to keep the stakes. [*Gives her a
  diamond.*]
Celinda.   'Tis done. [*Approaches the Cardinal.*]
Antonelli. [*Aside*] I have long had an appetite to this lady,
  But the lords keep her up so high—this toy   55
  May bring her on.
Cardinal. This interruption tastes not of good manners.
Celinda. But where necessity, my lord, compels,

53. *Gives her a diamond.*] *Subst. Forker; not in Oct.*   Approaches the
Cardinal.] *Subst. Gifford; not in Oct.*   54. *Aside*] *Walley; not in Oct.*

---

38. *sweat*] Cf. V.iii.205.
  pigeon's torment] mild punishment; cf. *Ham.*, II.ii.572; to be 'pigeon-liver'd
and lack gall' (the seat of ill-humour) is to be a coward.
  39. *a babe*] an innocent.
  40. *satisfied*] atoned for.
  44. *turtle*] turtle-dove, example of marital constancy (Tilley, T624) and of
patience (T573).
  45. *do . . . preferment*] act to her advantage.
  46.1. parchment] document on parchment.
  47.] Lawrence adds an aside but possibly Antonelli does not care if Celinda
hears him. See ll. 68–76.
  48. *is private*] by himself.
  55. *keep . . . high*] keep her arrogant by paying attention to her. 2 Lord (ll.
23–7) implies the opposite, and Celinda's own words (ll. 68–76) indicate that
she knows she's mocked.
  toy] trinket, or perhaps he means 'this foolish business of our wager'.

The boldness may meet pardon, and when you
Have found my purpose, I may less appear   60
Unmannerly.
Cardinal.   To th' business.
Celinda.   It did please
Your nephew, sir, before his death to credit me
With so much honourable favour, I
Am come to tender to his nearest of blood,
Yourself, what does remain a debt to him.   65
Not to delay your grace with circumstance,
That deed, if you accept, makes you my heir
Of no contemptible estate—   *He reads.*
            [Aside] this way
Is only left to tie up scurril tongues
And saucy men, that since Columbo's death   70
Venture to libel on my pride and folly;
His greatness and this gift which I enjoy
Still for my life, beyond which term a kingdom's
Nothing, will curb the giddy spleens of men
That live on impudent rhyme and railing at   75
Each wandering fame they catch.
Cardinal.   Madam, this bounty
Will bind my gratitude and care to serve you.
Celinda. I am your grace's servant.
Cardinal.   Antonelli—*Whisper.*
And when this noble lady visits me
Let her not wait.   80
Celinda. [*To Antonelli*] What think you, my officious sir; his
    grace

68. *Aside*] *Subst. Gifford; not in Oct.* 73. term a kingdom's] *Gifford;* term; a
Kingdom's, *Oct.* 81. *To Antonelli*] *Forker; not in Oct.* my officious sir;]
Subst. Gifford; my Officious, Sir; *Oct.*

69–70. *tie . . . men*] silence the scurrilous tongues of men like the lords and
Antonelli.
71. *libel on*] make rude comments about.
72. *His*] i.e. the Cardinal's.
72–3. *gift . . . life*] i.e. she loses nothing by making the Cardinal her heir.
75. *impudent rhyme*] scurrilous verses.
76. *Each wandering fame*] each reputation that has strayed from the
accepted path.
78. *Whisper.*] Perhaps the Cardinal arranges some reward for Celinda; or
perhaps he wants Antonelli to enlist her aid in his vengeance.

Is pleased, you may conjecture? I may keep
Your gem, the kiss was never yours.
Antonelli.   Sweet madam—
Celinda. Talk if you dare, you know I must not wait,
And so farewell for this time.   [*Exit.*]   85
Cardinal. [*Aside*] 'Tis in my brain already, and it forms
Apace, good, excellent revenge, and pleasant!
She's now within my talons; 'tis too cheap
A satisfaction for Columbo's death
Only to kill her by soft charm or force;   90
I'll rifle first her darling chastity,
'Twill be after time enough to poison her,
And she to th'world be thought her own destroyer.
As I will frame the circumstance, this night
All may be finished; for the colonel,   95
Her agent in my nephew's death, whom I
Disturbed at counsel with her, I may reach him
Hereafter, and be master of his fate.
We starve our conscience when we thrive in state.

                                        Exeunt.

ACT V, Scene ii

Enter ANTONIO *and* PLACENTIA.

Antonio. Placentia, we two are only left
Of my lady's servants, let us be true
To her and one another, and be sure
When we are at prayers, to curse the Cardinal.

---

85. *Exit.*] *Gifford; not in Oct.*   86. *Aside*] *Forker; not in Oct.*   0.1.
ANTONIO] *Gifford; Secretary Oct. (throughout scene).*

---

86. *'Tis . . . already*] For other plotters informing the audience of a new
scheme, see *Oth.*, I.iii.397–8, *White Devil*, IV.i.118ff., *Revenger's Tragedy*,
IV.ii.200–2.

90. *soft charm*] Either he envisages some magic potion or he imagines
beguiling the Duchess into a fatal situation.

91.] See Bowers, p. 229, for similar lustful villains.

94. *frame the circumstance*] organise the action.

96. *Her agent*] The Cardinal has not been entirely deceived by the
Duchess's madness.

whom] Hernando, who encountered the Cardinal in IV.ii.

Placentia. I pity my sweet lady.   5

Antonio. I pity her too, but am a little angry;
  She might have found another time to lose
  Her wits.

Placentia. That I were a man!

Antonio. What wouldst thou do, Placentia?   10

Placentia. I would revenge my lady.

Antonio. 'Tis better being a woman, thou mayst do
  Things that may prosper better, and the fruit
  Be thy own another day.

Placentia.   Your wit still loves
  To play the wanton.

Antonio.   'Tis a sad time, Placentia,   15
  Some pleasure would do well; the truth is, I
  Am weary of my life, and I would have
  One fit of mirth before I leave the world.

Placentia. Do not you blush to talk thus wildly?

Antonio. 'Tis good manners to be a little mad   20
  After my lady; but I ha' done. Who
  Is with her now?

Placentia.   Madam Valeria.

Antonio. Not Celinda? There's a lady for my humour,

20–2. 'Tis . . . Valeria.] *This ed.;* 'Tis . . . manners / To . . . Lady; / But . . . now?
/ Madam *Valeria.* / *Oct.*

5–11.] could be relined; I pity . . . pity / . . . might / . . . wits. / . . . do, /
. . . lady.

9.] Cf. *Ado*, IV.i.299ff., where Beatrice also longs for revenge.

12–14. *'Tis . . . day*] You do better as a woman since you can perform a
sexual act which unlike revenge may bear fruit (a child) which will be yours to
keep.

15. *play the wanton*] speak crudely.

16. *Some . . . well*] perhaps a pun on Placentia's name (Forker); the context
shows that Antonio longs for sexual pleasure.

18. *fit of mirth*] a sudden burst of enjoyment. A sexual meaning is unavoidable although the phrase was also used of a drinking bout (Beaumont
and Fletcher, *The Bloody Brother*, III.ii; *Wks.*, IV, 285).

19. *wildly*] (i) licentiously; (ii) distractedly. Antonio pretends to take the
second meaning.

21. *After*] in imitation of. See Nicolas Faret: a man must 'change his language and his maxime, according to the humour of those with whom chance
or his designes have ingaged him' (*The Honest Man: or, The Art to Please in
Court*, transl. by E(dward) G(rimstone), London, 1632, p. 169).

23. *Not Celinda*] We would not expect Celinda since the Duchess is no

A pretty book of flesh and blood, and well
Bound up, in a fair letter too; would I   25
Had her with all the errata.
Placentia.   She has not
An honourable fame.
Antonio.   Her fame? That's nothing,
A little stain, her wealth will fetch again
The colour, and bring honour into her cheeks
As fresh; if she were mine, and I had her   30
Exchequer, I know the way to make her honest,
Honest to th' touch, the test, and the last trial.
Placentia. How, prithee?
Antonio. Why, first I would marry her, that's a verb
material;
Then I would print her with an *Index*   35
Expurgatorius, a table drawn
Of her court heresies, and when she's read
Cum privilegio, who dares call her whore?

31. Exchequer, I] *Subst. Gifford;* Exchequer. I *Oct.*

---

longer on speaking terms with her, but she is introduced as an excuse for the
prurient jokes of ll. 32–8.

24. *book*] Cf. *Rom.*, I.iii.82–93.

25. *letter*] style of type.

26. *errata*] (i) printing faults; (ii) moral transgressions.

30. *As fresh*] as fresh as it was before the stain. The context hints at painted
colour and thus at a superficial honour.

31. *Exchequer*] her purse, which we know from V.i.67–8 is capacious.

32.] Antonio will establish her honour by testing it like gold.

touch] a test of the quality of gold or silver by rubbing it on a touchstone.

test] instrument on which refiners part gold and silver from other metals
(Blount, *Glossographia*, 1661).

trial] O.E.D., Try, vb., 3, 'to separate metal from dross'.

34. *that's . . . material*] (i) that's the important thing to do; (ii) that involves
physical activity.

35–6. Index /Expurgatorius] Authoritative list of passages to be deleted or
altered in works which a Roman Catholic could read once expurgated. 'Index'
could also mean 'pointer', i.e. 'phallus'; Antonio's would expunge previous
offences (Forker).

37. *court heresies*] In Celinda's case the passages to be omitted are her sexual
misdemeanours.

38. Cum privilegio] as in the booksellers' formula *Cum privilegio ad im-
primendum*, 'with the right to print'. 'Print' could mean 'impregnate' (cf.
Shakespeare, *Sonn*. 11, l. 14). The similar formula *Cum privilegio imprimendi*

Placentia. I'll leave you, if you talk thus.

Antonio.   I ha' done,
    Placentia, thou mayst be better company   40
    After another progress; and now tell me,
    Didst ever hear of such a patient madness
    As my lady is possessed with? She has raved
    But twice; and she would fright the Cardinal,
    Or at a supper if she did but poison him,   45
    It were a frenzy I could bear withal;
    She calls him her dear governor—

       Enter HERNANDO *disguised, having a letter.*

Placentia.   Who is this?

Hernando. Her secretary! Sir,
    Here is a letter, if it may have so
    Much happiness to kiss her grace's hand.   50

Antonio. From whom?

Hernando.   That's not in your commission, sir,
    To ask, or mine to satisfy; she will want
    No understanding when she reads.

Antonio.   Alas,
    Under your favour, sir, you are mistaken,
    Her grace did never more want understanding.   55

Hernando. How?

Antonio. Have you not heard? Her skull is broken, sir,
    And many pieces taken out, she's mad.

Hernando. The sad fame of her distraction
    Has too much truth it seems.

Placentia.   If please you, sir,   60

---

solum, 'with exclusive printing rights' (*O.E.D.*, Privilege, sb., 6) would suggest that when Antonio has exclusive rights to Celinda, no one will be able to
accuse her of dallying with other men.

    41. *progress*] state visit; loose conduct was common on such journeys
(Walley).

    42. *patient*] passive.

    47.1. disguised] Cf. the heroes in *Antonio's Revenge* and *Revenger's Tragedy*
(Forsythe). When Hernando confronts the Cardinal (V.iii.172.1), he is immediately recognised. Presumably, as in l. 69 below, his voice gives him away.

    49–50. *have . . . hand*] a common notion in Shirley's dedications.
Webster's dedications to *Duchess of Malfi, Devil's Law-Case* and *Monuments
of Honour* may have influenced Shirley (Forker).

    51. *That's . . . commission*] That's none of your business.

    52. *satisfy*] answer.

To expect awhile, I will present the letter.
Hernando. Pray do.   *Exit* PLACENTIA.
How long has she been thus distempered, sir?
Antonio. Before the Cardinal came to govern here,
Who for that reason by the king was made   65
Her guardian; we are now at his devotion.
Hernando. A lamb given up to a tiger! May diseases
Soon eat him through his heart!
Antonio.   Your pardon, sir,
I love that voice, I know it too, a little,
Are not you—be not angry, noble sir,   70
I can with ease be ignorant again,
And think you are another man, but if
You be that valiant gentleman they call—
Hernando. Whom? What?
Antonio. That killed—I would not name him if I thought   75
You were not pleased to be that very gentleman.
Hernando. Am I betrayed?
Antonio.   The devil sha' not
Betray you here; kill me, and I will take
My death you are the noble colonel;
We are all bound to you for the general's death,   80
Valiant Hernando! When my lady knows
You are here, I hope 'twill fetch her wits again;
But do not talk too loud, we are not all
Honest i'th' house, some are the Cardinal's creatures.
Hernando. Thou wert faithful to thy lady; I am glad   85
'Tis night—but tell me how the churchman uses
The Duchess.

---

66. *guardian*] The early Stuarts were particularly careless in granting to their followers both lunatics and their estates (Stone, p. 441).
at his devotion] under his command.
67. *A lamb . . . tiger!*] Cf. *The Imposture*, I.i: 'lamb yok'd with a tiger' (V,187); and Dekker, *Match Me in London*, V.ii.46–8: 'my Father swore / That I should marry thee, and then a Tyger / And a Lambe had beene together' (*Wks.*, III, 337).
69. *I love . . . know*] 'I agree with your sentiment and I begin to recognise your voice' (Forker). Or perhaps Antonio in his excitement anticipates his knowledge by stressing his delight in Hernando's presence.
78–9. *take . . . death*] swear on my death.
84. *Honest*] loyal.
creatures] puppets, tools.
85. *Thou*] a deliberate use of a more familiar address.

Enter ANTONELLI.

Antonio. He carries angels in his tongue and face, but I
    Suspect his heart; this is one of his spawns.
    Signor Antonelli.
Antonelli.   Honest Antonio.   90
Antonio. And how, and how—a friend of mine—where is
    The Cardinal's grace?
Hernando.   [*Aside*] That will be never answered.
Antonelli. He means to sup here with the Duchess.
Antonio.   Will he?
Antonelli. We'll have the charming bottles at my chamber;
    Bring that gentleman, we'll be mighty merry.   95
Hernando. [*Aside*] I may disturb your jollity.
Antonelli.   Farewell, sweet— [*Exit.*]
Antonio. Dear Antonelli—a round pox confound you.
    This is court rhetoric at the back stairs.

Enter PLACENTIA.

Placentia. Do you know this gentleman?
Antonio.   Not I.
Placentia. My lady presently dismissed Valeria,   100

---

92. *Aside*] Subst. *Gifford; not in Oct.*   96. *Aside*] Subst. *Gifford; not in*
Oct.   Exit.] *Gifford; not in Oct.*

87.1.] Antonelli, like the Cardinal, lurks in the background before
advancing.

88. *angels*] Cf. *H8*, III.i.145, where 'angels' faces' are contrasted with unknown 'hearts'.

89. *spawns*] offspring, i.e. followers; contemptuous.

91. *And . . . how*] Cf. *The Opportunity*, III.i; III, 405, and *The Imposture*,
V.i; V, 247; also Heywood and Brome, *The Late Lancashire Witches* (1634),
ed. Laird H. Barber, Garland Renaissance Drama (New York and London,
1979), l. 2750.

92. *grace*] (i) title accorded to dignitary; (ii) virtue.

94. *charming*] enchanting, in that they intoxicate. Frederick (*The Lady of
Pleasure*, III.ii; IV, 57), wants to drink 'T'other enchanted bottle'. The servants will have their own party while their masters feast.

96. *sweet*] a courtly affectation.

97. *round*] severe; perhaps a pun on the rhetorical sense, 'fluent' (Forker).

98. *court . . . stairs*] a sneer at Antonelli's aping of courtiers. For Shirley
court rhetoric almost invariably = insincerity and deception.

99–103.] Placentia may be expressing doubt about the propriety of this
interview, or may merely be curious as a result of the Duchess's reaction.

100. *presently*] immediately.

And bade me bring him to her bedchamber.

Antonio. The gentleman has an honest face.

Placentia.   Her words

Fell from her with some evenness and joy.

[*To Hernando*] Her grace desires your presence.

Hernando.   I'll attend her.

Exit [*with* PLACENTIA].

Antonio. I would this soldier had the Cardinal   105

Upon a promontory, with what a spring

The churchman would leap down; it were a spectacle

Most rare to see him topple from the precipice,

And souse in the salt water with a noise

To stun the fishes; and if he fell into   110

A net, what wonder would the simple sea-gulls

Have, to draw up the o'ergrown lobster,

So ready boiled! He shall have my good wishes;

This colonel's coming may be lucky. I

Will be sure none shall interrupt 'em.   115

Enter CELINDA.

Celinda. Is her grace at opportunity?

Antonio. No, sweet madam,

She is asleep, her gentlewoman says.

Celinda. My business is but visit, I'll expect.

102–3. *Her . . . joy*] *Gifford; one line in Oct.*   104. *To Hernando*] *Forker; not in Oct.   with* PLACENTIA] *Gifford; not in Oct.*

---

103. *evenness*] calmness.

108. *precipice*] Falling from or standing on a precipice is common in Shirley; cf. *The Doubtful Heir*, IV.i; IV, 325, *The Politician*, I.i; V, 98. 'Precipice' is also a favourite with Massinger.

109. *souse*] plunge into, literally 'put in pickle'. Cf. the Cardinal's abuse of Hernando in III.i.72; also *Malcontent*, IV.iii.46–7.

110–11. *fell . . . net*] The devil was sometimes described as a fisherman catching his prey like fish. See Thomas Adams, *The Blacke Devill* (London, 1615), pp. 40–1.

111. *sea-gulls*] foolish fishermen.

112–13. *o'ergrown . . . boiled*] another reference to the colour of the Cardinal's robes.

113. *He . . . wishes*] probably an ironic wish for the Cardinal. 'He' could just possibly be Hernando but it would then seem odd to describe him as 'This colonel' in the next line.

116. *at opportunity*] free to see me.

119. *expect*] wait.

Antonio. That must not be, although I like your company.   120
Celinda. You are grown rich, master secretary.
Antonio. I, madam? Alas!
Celinda. I hear you are upon another purchase.
Antonio. I upon a purchase?
Celinda.   If you want any sum—
Antonio. If I could purchase your sweet favour, madam?   125
Celinda. You shall command me and my fortune, sir.
Antonio. How's this?
Celinda.   I have observed you, sir, a staid
    And prudent gentleman—and I shall want—
Antonio. Not me?
Celinda. (*Aside*) A father for some infant; he has credit   130
    I'th' world; I am not the first cast lady
    Has married a secretary.
Antonio. Shall I wait upon you?
Celinda.   Whither?
Antonio.   Any whither.
Celinda. I may chance lead you then—
Antonio. I shall be honoured to obey; my blood   135
    Is up, and in this humour I'm for anything.
Celinda. Well, sir, I'll try your manhood.
Antonio.   'Tis my happiness,
    You cannot please me better.
Celinda.   [*Aside*] This was struck

---

130. *Aside*] Oct. prints in margin opposite l. *130*.   138. *Aside*] Subst. Gifford; not in Oct.

---

123. *upon . . . purchase*] about to make some new acquisition. Antonio is as puzzled as we are. Perhaps the reference is to Antonio's flirtation with Placentia, or to the offer of herself that Celinda is about to make (Forker). 'Purchase' could mean 'concubinage'.

130. *Aside*] Oct.'s s.d. may apply to all or only part of Celinda's speech. It is unlikely that she intends Antonio to hear any of her words and yet if the whole speech is an aside, 'I shall want–' is left hanging. Perhaps this is enough for Antonio to press home what he thinks is his advantage.

some infant] perhaps Columbo's child. He must have had a reason for leaving his fortune to Celinda. Yet any such relationship was hidden from the courtiers (V.i.23–5).

131. *cast*] discarded.

135–6. *blood . . . up*] Cf. V.iii.149.

137. *manhood*] manliness, with strong physical connotations.

138. *struck*] settled. Cf. 'strike a bargain'; also the proverb, 'strike while the iron is hot' (Forker).

I'th' opportunity.
Antonio.   I am made for ever.   [*Exeunt*.]

ACT V, SCENE iii

Enter HERNANDO *and* DUCHESS.

Hernando. Dear madam, do not weep.
Duchess.   Y'are very welcome;
    I ha' done, I wo' not shed a tear more
    Till I meet Alvarez, then I'll weep for joy;
    He was a fine young gentleman, and sung sweetly;
    And you had heard him but the night before   5
    We were married, you would ha' sworn he had been
    A swan, and sung his own sad epitaph;
    But we'll talk o' the Cardinal.
Hernando.   Would his death
    Might ransom your fair sense, he should not live
    To triumph in the loss; beshrew my manhood,   10
    But I begin to melt.
Duchess.   I pray, sir, tell me—
    For I can understand, although they say
    I have lost my wits; but they are safe enough,
    And I shall have 'em when the Cardinal dies,
    Who had a letter from his nephew too   15
    Since he was slain.
Hernando.   From whence?
Duchess. I know not where he is, but in some bower
    Within a garden he is making chaplets,
    And means to send me one, but I'll not take it;
    I have flowers enough I thank him while I live.   20

139. *Exeunt*.] Baskervill; *not in Oct.; Gifford gives separate exits.*

---

139. *I'th' opportunity*] to advantage.
  made] made fortunate. The Duchess is, in effect, deserted by Antonio.
  7. *swan*] believed to sing before death.
  10. *loss*] i.e. of her senses.
  beshrew] curse.
  11–16. *I pray . . . slain*] The Duchess confides her sanity to Hernando. The speeches that follow make some sense but, since she no longer needs to pretend madness, illustrate in their inconsequence and whimsy a genuine distraction.
  18. *chaplets*] garlands of flowers.

Hernando. But do you love your governor?

Duchess. Yes, but I'll never marry him, I am promised
    Already.

Hernando.   To whom, madam?

Duchess.   Do not you
    Blush when you ask me that, must not you be
    My husband? I know why, but that's a secret;   25
    Indeed if you believe me, I do love
    No man alive so well as you; the Cardinal
    Shall never know't, he'll kill us both, and yet
    He says he loves me dearly, and has promised
    To make me well again, but I'm afraid   30
    One time or other he will give me poison.

Hernando. Prevent him, madam, and take nothing from him.

Duchess. Why, do you think 'twill hurt me?

Hernando.   It will kill you.

Duchess. I shall but die, and meet my dear-loved lord,
    Whom when I have kissed, I'll come again, and work   35
    A bracelet of my hair for you to carry him,
    When you are going to heaven; the poesy shall
    Be my own name, in little tears, that I
    Will weep next winter, which congealed i'th' frost
    Will show like seed-pearl; you'll deliver it?   40
    I know he'll love and wear it for my sake.

Hernando. [*Aside*] She is quite lost.

---

42. *Aside*] *Forker; not in Oct.*

23–4. *Do . . . Blush*] an echo of Placentia's words at V.ii.19.

25. *why . . . secret*] She alludes to his killing of Columbo and his plan to kill
the Cardinal.

30–1. *I'm . . . poison*] a premonition which does not prevent her from eating
with the Cardinal.

35. *Whom . . . again*] when I have kissed him I'll come here again. Rosaura
wavers between life and death.

36. *bracelet . . . hair*] i.e. as a mourning bracelet. Cf. Donne's 'bracelet of
bright hair about the bone' ('The Relic', l. 6).

him] to him.

37. *poesy*] inscription. Perhaps a pun on 'posy' ('bouquet of flowers') in
reference to the derivation of Rosaura from *rosarius*, 'of roses' (Forker).

40. *seed-pearl*] Cf. IV.iii.54.

42. *quite lost*] echo of *White Devil*, I.ii.3. Hernando cannot believe the
Duchess is sane. Despite my s.d. these words may simply be his thoughts
spoken aloud, in the assumption that Rosaura is too far gone to understand

Duchess.   I pray give me, sir, your pardon,
  I know I talk not wisely, but if you had
  The burden of my sorrow, you would miss
  Sometimes your better reason; now I'm well;   45
  What will you do when the Cardinal comes?
  He must not see you for the world.
Hernando.   He sha' not,
  I'll take my leave before he come.
Duchess.   Nay stay,
  I shall have no friend left me when you go;
  He will but sup, he sha' not stay to lie wi' me;   50
  I have the picture of my lord abed,
  Three are too much this weather.

Enter PLACENTIA.

Placentia. Madam, the Cardinal.
Hernando. He shall sup with the devil.
Duchess.   I dare not stay,
  The red-cock will be angry; I'll come again.   55
               Exeunt [DUCHESS *and* PLACENTIA].

Hernando. This sorrow is no fable, now I find
  My curiosity is sadly satisfied;
  Ha! If the Duchess in her straggled wits
  Let fall words to betray me to the Cardinal,
  The panther will not leap more fierce to meet   60
  His prey, when a long want of food hath parched
  His starvèd maw, than he to print his rage
  And tear my heart-strings; everything is fatal,

55.1. DUCHESS *and* PLACENTIA.] *Gifford; not in Oct.*

---

him. She is not, and offers in ll. 43–5 a better explanation of her state of mind than she gave earlier.

  50. *he . . . me*] a bawdy joke which we know is close to the truth; a mild instance of the tendency to link madness and immodesty.

  52.] Cf. Beaumont and Fletcher, *Wit Without Money*, II.i: 'three in a Bed, Sir, will be too much this weather' (*Wks.*, II.165).

  55. *red-cock*] the Cardinal; 'cock' = 'one who arouses slumberers . . . applied to ministers of religion', 'chief person of a circle' (*O.E.D.*, 6, 7).

  57. *sadly*] grievously.

  58. *straggled*] wandering; a first appearance. See below, l. 197, and *Love in a Maze*, 'straggling senses', IV.iii; II, 341.

  60. *panther*] Cf. Shirley's *Narcissus*, VI, 476.

And yet she talked sometimes with chain of sense,
And said she loved me; ha! They come not yet;   65
I have a sword about me, and I left
My own security to visit death.
Yet I may pause a little, and consider
Which way does lead me to't most honourably;
Does not the chamber that I walk in tremble?   70
What will become of her, and me, and all
The world in one small hour? I do not think
Ever to see the day again; the wings
Of night spread o'er me like a sable hearse-cloth,
The stars are all close mourners too; but I   75
Must not alone to the cold, silent grave,
I must not; if thou canst, Alvarez, open
That ebon curtain, and behold the man,
When the world's justice fails shall right thy ashes,
And feed their thirst with blood; thy Duchess is   80
Almost a ghost already, and doth wear
Her body like a useless upper garment,
The trim and fashion of it lost. Ha!

Enter PLACENTIA.

Placentia. You need not doubt me, sir; my lady prays
    You would not think it long, she in my ear   85
    Commanded me to tell you that when last
    She drank, she had happy wishes to your health.
Hernando. And did the Cardinal pledge it?

---

64. *yet . . . sense*] Cf. Polonius' detecting of method in Hamlet's madness
(II.ii.204).

65. *They*] the Duchess and the Cardinal.

75. *close mourners*] deep mourners; probably originates in the seclusion of
mourners, i.e. 'close' in the sense of 'enclosed'. Cf. Shirley's elegy 'Upon the
death of King James' (VI, 445). Usage not recorded in *O.E.D.* before 1654.

76–7. *Must . . . not*] For similar repetition cf. *Love's Cruelty*, I.i: 'You shall
not go, indeed you shall not' (II, 193).

78. *the man*] the man who, i.e. Hernando.

81–2. *doth . . . garment*] an impressive image but often used by Shirley
(Bas, p. 383).

83. *trim and fashion*] Cf. Daniel's *Defence of Ryme* (1603), sig. G5.
Hernando seems to mean 'style and cut', i.e. the garment has become
shapeless.

85. *it*] i.e. the length of time she has been away.

86–7.] Rosaura reminds Hernando what is expected of him.

Placentia.   He was not
     Invited to't, nor must he know you are here.
Hernando. What do they talk of, prithee?   90
Placentia. His grace is very pleasant   *A lute is heard.*
     And kind to her, but her returns are after
     The sad condition of her sense, sometimes
     Unjointed.
Hernando.   They have music.
Placentia.   A lute only—
     His grace prepared, they say, the best of Italy—   95
     That waits upon my lord.
Hernando.   He thinks the Duchess
     Is stung with a tarantula.
Placentia.   Your pardon.
     My duty is expected.   *Exit.*
Hernando.   Gentle lady—
     A voice too?   *Song within.*
Strephon. Come, my Daphne, come away,   100
     We do waste the crystal day;
     'Tis Strephon calls.
Daphne.   What says my love?

93–4. The ... Unjointed] *Gifford; one line in Oct.*   94–5. only—/ ... prepared, ... Italy—] *This ed.;* only, / ... prepard, ... Italy / *Oct.;* only,/ ...
prepared; ... Italy,/ *Gifford;* only. / ... prepared, ... Italy, /
Baskervill.   98–9. Gentle ... too?] *Subst. Neilson; one line in Oct.*

---

    92. *returns*] replies.
    94. *Unjointed*] incoherent.
    94–6. *A lute ... lord*] ambiguous in Oct.; Gifford reads 'lute' as the object
of 'prepared'; Baskervill takes 'best of Italy' as the object and cuts off 'A lute
only' from the rest of the sentence.
    95. *best*] best player.
    97. *tarantula*] The tarantula's bite was popularly blamed for tarantism, a
disease (possibly hysterical) characterised by weeping, skipping about, and
frenzied dancing. It was common in parts of Italy from the fifteenth till the
seventeenth century. Dancing was seen variously as a cure or as a symptom
which had to be alleviated by special music or magic antidotes.
    voice] singer.
    100–18.] The music has survived. See Appendix III. There are minor
differences between the play's song text and that of Playford reproduced in
Appendix III. The version in *Poems, etc.* (1646) is different again in some
respects: 'would' for 'says' (l. 102); 'perfumed bosome', 'stray' for 'stay' (l.
112); 'this' for 'the' (l. 114). The song is parodied as a dialogue between Pluto
and Cromwell in *Rump; or An Exact Collection of the Choycest Poems and
Songs Relating to the Late Times* (1662), I, 339–40 (Armstrong, p. 60).

Strephon. Come follow to the myrtle grove,
    Where Venus shall prepare
    New chaplets for thy hair.   105
Daphne. Were I shut up within a tree,
    I'd rend my bark to follow thee.
Strephon. My shepherdess, make haste,
    The minutes slide too fast.
Daphne. In those cooler shades will I,   110
    Blind as Cupid, kiss thine eye.
Strephon. In thy bosom then I'll stay,
    In such warm snow who would not lose his way?
Daphne. We'll laugh and leave the world behind,
    And gods themselves that see,   115
    Shall envy thee and me;
        But never find
    Such joys, when they embrace a deity.
Hernando. If at this distance I distinguish, 'tis not
    Church music, and the air's wanton, and no anthem   120
    Sung to't, but some strange ode of love and kisses;
    What should this mean?—Ha, he is coming hither;
    I am betrayed, he marches in her hand;
    I'll trust a little more, mute as the arras,
    My sword and I here.   125
    He [draws his sword, hides behind the arras, and] observes.

    Enter CARDINAL, DUCHESS, ANTONELLI, *and* Attendants.

125.1. *draws his sword, hides behind the arras, and*] Subst. *Gifford who has
Hernando draw his sword at l. 122; not in* Oct.

---

   103. *myrtle grove*] especially associated with Venus.
   105. *chaplets*] Cf. V.iii.18.
   106–7.] an allusion to the nymph Daphne who was changed into a laurel
tree to protect her from her pursuer, Apollo.
   111. *Blind as Cupid*] The god of Love, son of Venus, was traditionally
blind.
   113. *warm snow*] also in *The Example*, IV.i; III, 332.
   119. *If . . . distinguish*] Cf. IV.ii.222–4.
   120. *Church . . . wanton*] Church music would be appropriate for a
Cardinal; instead the music is amorous.
   123. *in her hand*] holding her hand.
   124. *mute . . . arras*] Stage hangings provided a useful hiding-place in
Jacobean plays. Forsythe notes forty-one instances of eavesdropping in
Shirley (p. 92).

Cardinal. Wait you in the first chamber, and let none
    Presume to interrupt us.

                    Exeunt [ANTONELLI *and*] *Servants.*
                 [*Aside*] She is pleasant;
    Now for some art to poison all her innocence.

Duchess. [*Aside*] I do not like the Cardinal's humour; he
    Little suspects what guest is in my chamber.   130

Cardinal. Now, madam, you are safe.

Duchess.   How means your lordship?

Cardinal. [*Embracing her*] Safe in my arms, sweet Duchess.

Duchess.   Do not hurt me.

Cardinal. Not for the treasures of the world; you are
    My pretty charge, had I as many lives
    As I have careful thoughts to do you service,   135
    I should think all a happy forfeit to
    Delight your grace one minute; 'tis a heaven
    To see you smile.

Duchess.   What kindness call you this?

Cardinal. It cannot want a name while you preserve
    So plentiful a sweetness, it is love.   140

Duchess. Of me? How shall I know't, my lord?

Cardinal. By this, and this, swift messengers to whisper
    Our hearts to one another.   *Kisses* [*her*].

Duchess. Pray do you come a-wooing?

Cardinal.   Yes, sweet madam,
    You cannot be so cruel to deny me.   145

Duchess. What, my lord?

Cardinal.   Another kiss.

Duchess.   Can you
    Dispense with this, my lord? (*Aside*) Alas, I fear
    Hernando is asleep, or vanished from me.

Cardinal. [*Aside*] I have mocked my blood into a flame, and
    what

---

127. *Aside*] *Walley; not in Oct.*   127.1. ANTONELLI *and*] *Gifford; not in
Oct.*   127-8. *She ... innocence.*] *Gifford; one line in Oct.*   129. *Aside*]
Walley; not in Oct.   132. *Embracing her*] *Subst. Gifford; not in Oct.*   143.
her] *Gifford; not in Oct.*   149. *Aside*] *Subst. Gifford; not in Oct.*

---

126. *first chamber*] antechamber.
128. *poison*] He will corrupt the Duchess and then literally poison her.
131. *safe*] (i) protected; (ii) unable to escape.
138. *kindness*] (i) kind act; (ii) affection.
143. *Our hearts*] our emotions.

My angry soul had formed for my revenge   150
Is now the object of my amorous sense;
I have took a strong enchantment from her lips,
And fear I shall forgive Columbo's death
If she consent to my embrace; [*To her*] come, madam.
Duchess. Whither, my lord.
Cardinal.   But to your bed or couch,   155
Where if you will be kind, and but allow
Yourself a knowledge, Love, whose shape and raptures
Wise poets have but glorified in dreams,
Shall make your chamber his eternal palace;
And with such active and essential streams   160
Of new delights glide o'er your bosom, you
Shall wonder to what unknown world you are
By some blest change translated; why d'ye pause?
And look so wild? Will you deny your governor?
Duchess. How came you by that cloven foot?
Cardinal.   Your fancy   165
Would turn a traitor to your happiness;
I am your friend, you must be kind.
Duchess.   Unhand me,
Or I'll cry out a rape.
Cardinal.   You wo' not sure?
Duchess. [*Aside*] I have been cozened with Hernando's
        shadow;
Here's none but heaven to hear me—help, a rape!   170

---

155. couch,] *Corr. Oct.;* couch / *uncorr. Oct.*   156. kind, and] *Corr. Oct.;*
kind and *uncorr. Oct.*   157. raptures /] *Corr. Oct.;* raptures, *uncorr.*
Oct.   158. dreams,] *Corr. Oct.;* dreams. *uncorr. Oct.*   163. d'ye] *Brooke;*
d'e *Oct.*   169. *Aside*] *Walley; not in Oct.*

155–63. *But . . . translated*] Other notable instances of an unexpected
seducer include Volpone, and Angelo in *Meas.* Both, like the Cardinal, are
resisted by angry chastity.

160. *essential*] concentrated, with a suggestion of perfume ('essence').

162. *unknown world*] ominous, given the play's earlier reference to the 'unknown other world', I.ii.82.

165. *cloven foot*] identifies the Cardinal with the devil. Cf. *Oth.*,
V.ii.289–90; also often in Shirley, e.g. *The Bird in a Cage*, II.i; II, 388, *The
Grateful Servant*, IV.v; II, 77.

167. *kind*] The Cardinal twists the sense from 'friendly' to 'loving'. See
l. 138.

Cardinal. Are you so good at understanding? Then
 I must use other argument.

      He forces her. [*Hernando leaps out.*]
Hernando.   Go to,
 Cardinal!

            Strikes him.
            Exit DUCHESS.

Cardinal. Hernando, murder, treason, help!
Hernando. An army sha' not rescue thee; your blood
 Is much inflamed, I have brought a lancet wi' me   175
 Shall open your hot veins and cool your fever;
 To vex thy parting soul, it was the same
 Engine that pinced Columbo's heart. [*Stabs him.*]
Cardinal.   Help, murder!

   Enter ANTONELLI *and* Servants.

Antonelli. Some ring the bell, 'twill raise the court;
 My lord is murdered, 'tis Hernando. *The bell rings.* 180
Hernando. I'll make you all some sport—
   [*In the ensuing scuffle, Hernando is wounded.*]

        So, now we are even.
 Where is the Duchess? I would take my leave
 Of her, and then bequeath my curse among you.

          Hernando falls.

171. understanding? Then] *Subst. Gifford;* understanding then,
Oct. 172.1. *Hernando leaps out.*] *Subst. Gifford; not in Oct.* 172–3. Go to,
/ Cardinal!] *This ed.; one line in Oct.* 178. pinced] pinc'd *Oct.;* pierced
Gifford. Stabs him.] *Gifford; not in Oct.* 181.1.] *Subst. Lawrence; not in
Oct.; stabs himself. Gifford.*

 171.] So you are not too mad to know what's going on.
 172.1. forces] can = 'ravish', but l. 193 shows that matters don't go this far;
he overpowers her with violence and is about to rape her.
 Hernando . . . out] Cf. Bonario in *Volpone*, III.vii.
 175–6. *Lancet . . . fever*] an image from blood-letting, the treatment for
fever.
 178. *pinced*] a variant of 'pinched'. Forker is the first ed. to retain this verb,
instead of emending to 'pierced'.
 179. *ring the bell*] See Introduction, p. 26.
 181.1.] All edd. apart from Lawrence follow Gifford here. Lawrence takes
his cue from Frank Manley (*N.& Q.*, N.S., XII, 1965, 342–3), who argues
that Hernando had seemed eager to live to enjoy the Duchess and anxious to
protect his own life. The sport he offers is a fight (see IV.iii.16), and in scuf-
fling with Antonelli and the servants he dies.
 181. *now . . . even*] We've settled accounts. Cf. IV.iii.71.

Enter KING, DUCHESS, VALERIA, Lords, Guard.

King. How come these bloody objects?

Hernando. With a trick my sword found out; I hope he's
    paid.   185

1 Lord. [*Aside*] I hope so too—a surgeon for my lord
    Cardinal.

King. Hernando!

Duchess. Justice, O justice, sir, against a ravisher.

Hernando. Sir, I ha' done you service.

King.   A bloody service.

Hernando. 'Tis pure scarlet.   190

Enter Surgeon.

Cardinal. [*Aside*] After such care to perfect my revenge,
    Thus bandied out o'th' world by a woman's plot?

Hernando. I have preserved the Duchess from a rape;
    Goodnight to me and all the world for ever.   *Dies.*

King. [*To Cardinal*] So impious?

Duchess.   'Tis most true, Alvarez' blood   195
    Is now revenged; I find my brain return,
    And every straggling sense repairing home.

Cardinal. I have deserved you should turn from me, sir,
    My life hath been prodigiously wicked,
    My blood is now the kingdom's balm; O sir,   200
    I have abused your ear, your trust, your people,
    And my own sacred office, my conscience
    Feels now the sting; O show your charity,
    And with your pardon like a cool, soft gale
    Fan my poor sweating soul, that wanders through   205

---

186. *Aside*] *Neilson; not in Oct.*   191. *Aside*] *Subst. Gifford; not in*
Oct.

---

184. *bloody objects*] Hernando and the Cardinal.

190. *pure scarlet*] i.e. bloody, but sinless (Forker).

194.] See V.iii.73, and *The Maid's Revenge*, IV.iv; I, 174; also *R3*, IV.iii.39.

197. *straggling*] See V.iii.58.

200. *balm*] Cf. *Love in a Maze*, III.iii: II, 326, and *The Grateful Servant*,
I.ii; II, 17, where 'blood' and 'balm' appear close together. Cf. also *Changeling*, V.iii.150–1.

201. *I . . . ear*] Cf. the Duchess's accusations, II.iii.145–7.

205. *sweating*] See V.i.38.

Unhabitable climes and parchèd deserts;
[*To Duchess*] But I am lost, if the great world forgive
   me,
Unless I find your mercy for a crime
You know not, madam, yet against your life.
I must confess more than my black intents   210
Upon your honour, y'are already poisoned.
King. By whom?
Cardinal. By me;
   In the revenge I owed Columbo's loss,
   With your last meat was mixed a poison that   215
   By subtle and by sure degrees must let in death.
King. Look to the Duchess, our physicians!
Cardinal. Stay, I will deserve her mercy, though I cannot
   Call back the deed; in proof of my repentance,
   If the last breath of a now dying man   220
   May gain your charity and belief, receive
   This ivory box, in it an antidote
   'Bove that they call the great magistral medicine;
   That powder mixed with wine by a most rare
   And quick access to the heart will fortify it   225
   Against the rage of the most nimble poison;
   I am not worthy to present her with it,
   O take it and preserve her innocent life.
1 Lord. Strange, he should have a good thing in such
   readiness.

---

207. *To Duchess*] *Forker; not in Oct.*   209–10. / I . . . confess more] *Brooke;*
life. / I . . . confess, more *Oct.;* life, / I . . . confess, more *Gifford.*   216. let
in death] *Oct.;* let / In death *Gifford.*

---

206. *unhabitable*] uninhabitable.
208–10.] Oct.'s comma after 'confess' is confusing. I follow Brooke, Forker
and Lawrence in omitting it. Gifford and all other edd. repunctuate more
radically so that 'more than my black intents' goes with 'a crime . . . against
your life', with 'I must confess' virtually in parenthesis. This reading makes
less sense than Oct.'s.
215. *meat*] food.
217.] Cf. *The Politician*, V.ii: 'Look to Albina. Our physicians!' (V, 172).
223. *magistral*] supremely effective.
228. *take it*] Perhaps a servant should leave the stage with the box to re-
enter '*with* . . . *wine*' at l. 234.1; or perhaps the Cardinal adds the powder to
the wine.
229.] a hint that all may not be well. Yet the Cardinal's 'readiness' is not

Cardinal. 'Tis that which in my jealousy and state,   230
    Trusting to false predictions of my birth,
    That I sho' die by poison, I preserved
    For my own safety; wonder not I made
    That my companion was to be my refuge.

        Enter Servant *with a bowl of wine.*

1 Lord. Here's some touch of grace.   235
Cardinal. In greater proof of my pure thoughts I take
    This first, and with my dying breath confirm
    My penitence; it may benefit her life,
    But not my wounds; [*Drinks.*] O hasten to preserve her,
    And though I merit not her pardon, let not   240
    Her fair soul be divorced.

                             [*Duchess drinks.*]

King.   This is some charity;
    May it prosper, madam.
Valeria.   How does your grace?
Duchess. And must I owe my life to him whose death
    Was my ambition? Take this free acknowledgement,
    I had intent this night with my own hand   245
    To be Alvarez' justicer.
King.   You were mad,
    And thought past apprehension of revenge.

230. 'Tis] *Gifford;* This *Oct.*   232. sho'] *Forker;* sh *Oct.*   239. *Drinks.*]
Go:se; not in Oct.   241.1.] *Subst. Gifford; not in Oct.*   241–2. This . . .
madam.] *This ed.; one line in Oct.*

---

altogether strange; intriguing courtiers lived in fear of poisoning (Fredson
Bowers, *J.E.G.P.*, xxxvi, 1937, 491–504, p. 503).

    230. *'Tis that*] Gifford's emendation makes sense of clumsiness. 'This'
seems a compositor's error, either through attraction of *th* from 'that' or from
misreading of ''Tis' (Forker).

    jealousy] fear of evil.

    and state] the status giving rise to such fears, or possibly the whole phrase
means 'apprehensive state' (Forker).

    231. *of*] at.

    232. *sho'*] Given Shirley's characteristic contractions (notably 'wo'' for
'would'), omission of *o* seems the most likely mistake here.

    233. *I made*] that I made.

    234. *was*] which was.

    241. *divorced*] i.e. from her body.

    246. *justicer*] occurs in *Lr.*, IV.ii.79, as 'vindicator of right'. The Duchess
attributes justice to revenge.

    247. *thought . . . revenge*] thought incapable of considering revenge.

Duchess. That shape I did usurp, great sir, to give
    My art more freedom and defence, but when
    Hernando came to visit me, I thought   250
    I might defer my execution,
    Which his own rage supplied without my guilt,
    And when his lust grew high, met with his blood.
1 Lord. The Cardinal smiles.
Cardinal.   Now my revenge has met
    With you, my nimble Duchess; I have took   255
    A shape to give my act more freedom too,
    And now I am sure she's poisoned with that dose
    I gave her last.
King.   Th'art not so horrid!
Duchess. Ha! Some cordial.
Cardinal.   Alas, no preservative
    Hath wings to overtake it; were her heart   260
    Locked in a quarry, it would search and kill
    Before the aids can reach it; I am sure
    You sha' not now laugh at me.
King. How came you by that poison?
Cardinal.   I prepared it,
    Resolving when I had enjoyed her, which   265
    The colonel prevented, by some art
    To make her take it, and by death conclude

---

248. I did usurp] *2nd stage corr. Oct.;* I did usurpe *uncorr. Oct.;* I did usurpe *1st stage corr. Oct.*   252. own] *Gifford;* owe *Oct.*   supplied] suppli'd *corr. Oct.;* supplide *uncorr. Oct.*   258. horrid!] *Walley;* horrid. *uncorr. Oct.;* horrid? *corr. Oct.*   259. Ha!] *Corr. Oct.;* Ha? *uncorr. Oct.*

---

   248. *shape*] technical term for stage dress or theatrical role; also a more general term for disguise.
   249. *art*] deception.
   250–3. *I . . . blood*] I thought I might hand over ('defer') the execution of revenge to Hernando who was angry enough without any guilty promptings from me. When the Cardinal's lust boiled over ('grew high') it was quenched by his own spilled blood.
   255–6. *took . . . freedom*] The Cardinal picks up the Duchess's words of ll. 248–9.
   257. *dose*] specific quantity of drug. Gotharus in *The Politician*, IV.iv, is poisoned with a box of 'medicine' (V, 154).
   258. *horrid*] causing horror, detestable.
   261. *Locked . . . quarry*] Cf. IV.ii.59–63.

My last revenge; you have the fatal story.

King. This is so great a wickedness, it will
    Exceed belief.

Cardinal.   I knew I could not live.   270

Surgeon. Your wounds, sir, were not desperate.

Cardinal.   Not mortal, ha?
    Were they not mortal?

Surgeon.   If I have skill in surgery.

Cardinal. Then I have caught myself in my own engine.

2 Lord. It was your fate, you said, to die by poison.

Cardinal. That was my own prediction to abuse   275
    Your faith; no human art can now resist it,
    I feel it knocking at the seat of life,
    It must come in; I have wracked all my own
    To try your charities, now it would be rare,
    If you but waft me with a little prayer,   280
    My wings that flag may catch the wind; but 'tis
    In vain, the mist is risen, and there's none
    To steer my wandering bark.   *Dies.*

1 Lord.   He's dead!

King.   With him
    Die all deceivèd trust.

2 Lord. This was a strange impiety.

King.   When men   285
    Of gifts and sacred function once decline

---

268. story.] Story. *2nd stage corr. Oct.;* Story? *uncorr. and 1st stage corr.*
Oct.   271–2. Your . . . surgery.] *This ed.;* Your . . . desperate. / Not . . . mor-
tall? / If . . . Surgery. *Oct.;* Your . . . mortal? / Ha . . . surgery. *Baskervill.*

271–2. *desperate . . . I have . . . surgery*] See my comment on elision in
Introduction, p. 31.

272. *If*] i.e. not if.

273. *caught . . . engine*] a stock situation in revenge plays. Shirley echoes
White Devil, V.vi.123–4: 'Thou art caught– / In thine own engine.'

275. *abuse*] take advantage of.

278–9. *wracked . . . charities*] I have destroyed my own charitable impulses
(i.e. in behaving as I have) in order to put your charity to the test.

279. *it . . . rare*] Cf. III.ii.112. The Cardinal enjoys tight situations.

279–80.] Note the rhyme. Perhaps the Cardinal pauses as if ending here,
then recovers to say more.

281. *flag*] become feeble in flight.

282–3. *mist . . . bark*] See I.ii.239n. The comparison of a disturbed spirit to
a traveller in bad weather is common. Cf. I.i.38–49; also *White Devil*,
V.vi.248–60.

From virtue, their ill deeds transcend example.
Duchess. The minute's come that I must take my leave too.
　　Your hand, great sir, and though you be a king,
　　We may exchange forgiveness. Heaven, forgive,　　290
　　And all the world! I come, I come, Alvarez!　　*Dies.*
King. Dispose their bodies for becoming funeral;
　　How much are kings abused by those they take
　　To royal grace! Whom, when they cherish most
　　By nice indulgence, they do often arm　　295
　　Against themselves; from whence this maxim springs,
　　None have more need of perspectives than kings.　　*Exeunt.*

---

　　291. *all . . . world*] appears for the third time in this scene; see ll. 71–2 and 194.
　　I . . . Alvarez!] Cf. *The Traitor*, V.iii: 'I am coming Amidea, I am coming' (II, 183), and *Ant.*, V.ii.285.
　　292. *becoming*] fitting.
　　293. *How . . . abused*] perhaps another allusion to Charles's political difficulties (Forker).
　　295. *nice*] weak (*O.E.D.*, 4c, 'not able to endure much; tender, delicate').
　　296. *maxim*] Shirley draws attention to the gnomic nature of his final line.

Epilogue

[*Voice*] *within.* Master Pollard, where's master Pollard for
    the epilogue?

    He [*Mr Pollard, as Epilogue*] *is thrust upon the stage, and
        falls.*

Epilogue. I am coming to you, gentlemen, the poet
    Has helped me thus far on my way, but I'll
    Be even with him; the play is a tragedy,   5
    The first that ever he composed for us,
    Wherein he thinks he has done prettily,

                Enter Servant.

    And I am sensible—[*To Servant*] I prithee look,
    Is nothing out of joint? Has he broke nothing?
Servant. No, sir, I hope.   10
Epilogue. Yes, he has broke his epilogue all to pieces;
    Canst thou put it together again?
Servant.   Not I, sir.

1. *Voice*] Baskervill; not in Oct.   3–26.] *In italics in Oct.*   8. *To Servant*]
Forker; not in Oct.

EPILOGUE] an early instance of a tragedy with comic epilogue (Forsythe,
p. 189).

    1. *Pollard*] Thomas Pollard, who was already playing comic parts in 1623;
his roles include Pinac and the Lieutenant in Beaumont and Fletcher's *Wild
Goose-Chase* and *Humorous Lieutenant*. He died between 1648 and 1655.
Theophilus Bird claimed he seized playhouse books and effects and sold them
for his own gain after 1642, but Bentley disputes this allegation (Bentley, II,
532–5).
    6.] i.e. the first tragedy for the King's Men. See Introduction, p. 1.
    7.] See Dedication, l. 11, and Prologue, l. 24.
    8. *sensible*] 'aware', with a hint of 'endowed with sensation' which he takes
up when the servant interrupts him.
    11.] The implication is that it is the author (l. 1) who called anxiously for the
epilogue; he has now damaged the speaker and as a result spoiled the speech.

Epilogue. Nor I, prithee be gone;

[*Exit* Servant.]

hum! Master poet,

I have a teeming mind to be revenged.

[*To audience*] You may assist, and not be seen in't now,   15

If you please, gentlemen, for I do know

He listens to the issue of his cause;

But blister not your hands in his applause;

Your private smile, your nod, or hum, to tell

My fellows, that you like the business well;   20

And when without a clap you go away,

I'll drink a small-beer health to his second day;

And break his heart, or make him swear and rage,

He'll write no more for the unhappy stage;

But that's too much, so we should lose; faith show it,   25

And if you like his play, 't's as well he knew it.

FINIS.

13.1. *Exit* Servant.] *Subst. Gifford; not in Oct.*   15. *To audience*] *Baskervill;
not in Oct.*   now,] *Gifford;* now. *Oct.*

---

14. *a teeming . . . revenged*] a mind breeding revenge. See Abbot, § 419a.

15. To audience] but just possibly he still addresses, ironically, the author.
See l. 11.

not . . . in't] without appearing to do so.

17. *issue . . . cause*] He implies that the author is on trial.

19–20.] alternatives to clapping which will presumably satisfy the actors
but not the dramatist listening in the wings (although 'hum' is usually a
dissatisfied exclamation).

21. *without a clap*] 'a pun on the venereal disease with reference to the
serious (as opposed to licentious) subject matter of the play' (Forker). If
Forker is right, the pun's presence introduces a trace of the wantonness which
Shirley claims to reject.

22. *small . . . day*] Small beer was thin and weak. The health drunk is thus
contemptuous and half-hearted. 'Second day' refers not just to further performances but to a benefit performance for the author (Bentley, *Profession*,
pp. 130–4).

24.] As the last words must have reminded the Blackfriars audience whose
theatre was frequently attacked by its Puritan neighbours, such a threat might
recoil on the dramatist. By 2 September of the following year the theatres
were closed, and Shirley's last play, *The Court Secret*, was for a long time
unstaged.

25. *lose*] i.e. forfeit our earnings.

A. COPIES OF OCTAVO CONSULTED
(abbreviations as in Wing)

Bodleian Library 8°B 13 Art BS	O1.	
Bodleian Library Douce 569	O2.	
Bodleian Library Mal. 256	O3.	
British Museum 1346.b.34	Ll.	
British Museum c.12.f.19	L2.	
British Museum 18,784	L3.	
British Museum E1226	L4.	microfilm
Cambridge University	C.	
Leeds University	Leeds.	
National Library of Scotland H.30.f.13	EN1.	
National Library of Scotland H.3.d.5	EN2.	
Victoria and Albert Museum	LV.	
Worcester College, Oxford	OW.	
Boston Public Library	MB.	
Columbia University, New York	NC.	microfilm
Cornell University	NIC.	xerox
Duke University	Duke.	microfilm
Folger Shakespeare Library CB824	WF1.	microfilm
Folger Shakespeare Library CB1271	WF2.	microfilm
Harvard University 14433.30.22	MH1.	
Harvard University 14433.30.30	MH2	
Huntington Library 147757	CH1.	microfilm
Huntington Library 146316	CH2.	microfilm
Library of Congress	LC.	microcard
McMaster University B10155	McMU1.	
McMaster University B10201	McMU2.	
McMaster University B10202	McMU3.	
McMaster University B10203	McMU4.	
McMaster University B10204	McMU5.	
McMaster University B10205	McMU6.	
Newberry Library	CN.	microfilm
New York Public Library	NN.	
Princeton University Ex.		

3930.3.323	NP1.	
Princeton University Ex.		
3930.3.386	NP2.	
R. H. Taylor Collection, at		
Princeton	Taylor.	
University of California, Los		
Angeles *PR 3144 C21	UCLA1.	microfilm
University of Chicago	CU.	microfilm
University of Illinois	IU.	microfilm
University of Indiana	INU.	microfilm
University of Michigan	MU.	microfilm
University of Pennsylvania	PU.	xerox
Williams College	WCL.	
Yale University	Y.	

Proof-corrections have been checked for me in the following copies:

Bibliothèque Nationale, Paris	BN.
Turnbull Library, New	
Zealand	NZ.
University of California, Los	
Angeles *PR 3142 A1 1653	UCLA2.

B. PROOF-CORRECTIONS

Outer B
Uncorrected: EN1, CH2.
Corrected: all other copies.

	uncorr.	corr.
B2v l. 34	shees	shee's
B3 l. 8	is, (I	is (I
B3 l. 20	grim /	grim-
B3 l. 23	talk /	talk,
B4v l. 26	thoughts,	thoughts;
B8v l. 10	face of	face, of (comma turned)

Forker thinks that on B4v uncorr. copies have 'Card.' in l. 25 while corr. copies have 'Card', but since several corr. copies have 'Card.' it seems more likely that during printing the full stop slipped and no longer showed.

Inner B
Uncorrected: EN1, CH2, McMU2.
Corrected: all other copies.

	uncorr.	corr.
B2 l. 7	*Arragonians* /	*Arragonians,*

B2 l. 15	crime.	crime?
B4 l. 8	happiness,—	happiness—
B4	No sig.	B4
B6 l. 6	worlds,	worlds /
B7v l. 6	speak.	speak,
B8 l. 22	insolent,	insolent!

Several copies (O2, L2, Leeds, MB, WF2, IU, PU, WCL, UCLA2) have 'speak /' on sig. B7v. Forker found this reading in WF2 and comments 'punctuation missing, probably uninked'. What happened becomes clear if we link the variation with what happens to 'motive' on sig. B6 (l. 12). In all uncorr. copies the reading is 'motive'. In corr. copies the reading is variously 'motive' (INU), 'mot ive' (MU), and 'mo tive' (NIC). The copies with 'speak /' all have 'mo tive'. None of the 'speak /' copies has the faintest hint of the missing comma. The change from 'motive' to 'mot ive' to 'mo tive' indicates that B6 was not adequately tightened after the correction of 'worlds,' was effected. It looks as though the same was true of B7v after the change from 'speak.' to 'speak,'. The relatively high number of copies without the comma suggests that the punctuation was not merely uninked but had dropped out, although there is always the slight possibility that 'speak/' represents a further proof-correction.

Outer C

Uncorrected: L1, NC.
1st stage correction: McMU6.
2nd stage correction: all other copies.

	uncorr.	1st stage	2nd stage
C2v l. 32	pretentions	pretentions	pretensions
C3 l. 1	weat	what	what
C6v l. 24	plack batch	black patch	black patch

Forker, working from microfilm, records an uncorrected inner C in LC. I have seen LC in microcard. The copy is badly inked but on C4 l. 29 where Forker records no punctuation after 'Mariage' there is faint punctuation which may well be a blemished reproduction of the comma in all other copies. Forker's other 'corrections' are consistent with the poor printing of inner C in LC. I think this forme represents an inferior pull rather than a single uncorrected copy.

Inner D

Uncorrected: NP1, CU, INU.
1st stage correction: O3, L3, EN2, LV, NC, Duke, WF1, MH1,

CH1, McMU1, 3, 5 and 6, CN, UCLA1, BN, NZ.
2nd stage correction: all other copies.

	uncorr.	1st stage	2nd stage
D1v l. 17	ransom'd;	ransom'd;	ransom'd,
D3v l. 14	her,	her,	her.
D3v l. 21	powerfull /	powerfull /	powerfull,
D3v l. 27	mmch	much	much
D4 l. 24	prevail'd,	prevail'd,	prevail'd.
D6 l. 27	sacrifice	sacrifice	sacrifise
D7v l. 8	cannot /	cannot/	cannot,
D7v l. 9	distance you	distance you	distance;
D7v l. 20	Uunfortunate,	Uunfortunate,	Uunfortunate;
D7v l. 34	me, 'tis	me, 'tis	me 'tis
D8 l. 13	punishment,	punishment,	punishment.
D8 l. 16	blody	blody	bloody
D8 l. 22	tears.	tears.	tears, / Hereafter—

The corrections are accompanied by a loosening of letters on D1v, l. 16. Uncorr. 'severall' becomes 'sever all' in corrected copies.

Inner and Outer E

No proof-correction but once again LC is less well inked than all other copies.

Outer F

Uncorrected: O3, EN2, McMU1 and 3, NP1, CU, INU (sig. F1 missing), UCLA2.
1st stage correction: O2, L1, PU, WCL.
2nd stage correction: all other copies.

	uncorr.	1st stage	2nd stage
F1 l. 18	couch /	couch,	couch,
F1 l. 19	kind and	kind, and	kind, and
F1 l. 20	raptures,	raptures /	raptures /
F1 l. 21	dreams.	dreams,	dreams,
F2v l. 15	Idid usurpe	I did usurpe	I did usurp
F2v l. 19	supplide	suppli'd	suppli'd
F2v l. 27	horrid.	horrid?	horrid?
F2v l. 28	Ha?	Ha!	Ha!
F3 l. 3	Story?	Story?	Story.

The only proof-correction apparent in the copies consulted by Forker is the change in the catchword on F3 which he guesses is

corrected from *E pilogue* to *Epilogue*. The other proof-corrections
indicate that this is not a correction but a deterioration. Uncorr.
copies have *Epilogue* with *E* either intact or broken. 1st stage corr.
copies all have *Epilogue* with broken *E*. 2nd stage corr. copies have
Epilogue or *E pilogue*, both with broken *E*.

Inner F

Forker records one proof-correction on F2, from 'Dutchess;' to
'Dutchess,' (l. 17). I have detected 'Dutchess;' in two copies, one
WF2 which both Forker and I have seen in microfilm, one C of which
I have seen the original. In both, the upper part of the semi-colon
looks more like a mark or flaw in the paper. I think this is a ghost
correction.

APPENDIX II
The alternative prologue

These verses are printed as the '*Prologue to his Tragedy call'd* the
Cardinall' in Shirley's *Poems, etc.* (1646), but in *Six New Playes*, they
appear as the prologue to *The Sisters*. 'London is gone to York' (l. 14)
tells us that this cannot be *The Cardinal*'s original prologue; the king
left London on 3 March 1642 and reached York on 19 March. *The
Cardinal* must originally have been performed shortly after its licens-
ing in November 1641. *The Sisters*, licensed on 26 April 1642, more
closely fits the references in this prologue.

Gifford thinks this was the original *Cardinal* prologue, that it was
transferred to *The Sisters*, and that a new prologue was given to *The
Cardinal* in 1652. This explanation does not account for the probable
reference to Richelieu in l. 3 of the present prologue which dates it no
later than 1642. Armstrong thinks the alternative prologue was composed for a production of *The Cardinal* in 1642, and was transferred
to *The Sisters*. He too thinks the present prologue came later, but also
in 1642. Both Bentley (V, 1148) and Forker think the alternative
prologue was originally written for *The Sisters* and revised for a summer production of *The Cardinal*. Greg suggests a mistake in the
Poems attribution, but Forker dismisses this explanation since
Armstrong demonstrates Shirley's care in the poems. Bentley and
Forker are almost certainly right. There is one other (slight) possibility. This prologue was originally composed for *The Sisters*. Line
20 suggests that it was folly to restage an old play, which tells against

a revival of *The Cardinal*. Perhaps Shirley did not make a mistake but deliberately printed a prologue which stands on its own as a poem better than the present *Cardinal* prologue does—but attached it to his favourite play.

My text is based on the version in *Poems, etc.*

Does this look like a term? I cannot tell.
Our poet thinks the whole town is not well,
Has took some physic lately, and for fear
Of catching cold, dares not salute this air.
How like a withered and forsaken place   5
Hath this appeared! No influence, no grace
From any star, as nature meant to be
At loss and show here dwelt vacuity:
As time, with age turned child, had got a fall,
Broken a limb, and lost his usual   10
Motion, which strikes a lameness in the year,
We are to have but little summer here.
But now I guess the reason, I hear say
London is gone to York, 'tis a great way;
Pox o' the proverb and of him, say I,   15
That looked o'er Lincoln; 'cause that was, must we
Be now translated north? I could rail too
On Gammer Shipton's ghost but't wo' not do,
The town will still be flecking and a play,
Though ne'er so new, starves now the second day.   20
Upon these very hard conditions,
Our poet will not purchase many towns,
And if you leave us too, we cannot thrive;

1. like] *Oct.; not in Poems, etc.*   5–12.] *Poems, etc.; not in Oct.*   13. now . . .
reason] *Poems, etc.;* ther's another reason *Oct.*   20. starves now] *Poems, etc.;*
will starve *Oct.*

---

1. *term*] period when the law-courts were in session and London could be expected to be busy.

14. *London . . . York*] See introductory comment, above.

15–16. *Pox . . . Lincoln*] proverbial reference to the devil; Tilley D277.

18. *Gammer Shipton's ghost*] Mother Shipton was a prophetess, born in 1488 but first recorded in a pamphlet in 1641. She was said to have forecast several important deaths, including Wolsey's. Armstrong, p. 75, quotes one of her prophecies: 'the Kingdome shall be governed by 3 Lords, and then *Yorke* shall be London'.

19. *flecking*] flitting, fluttering about.

20. *second day*] See Epilogue, l. 22n.

I'll promise neither play nor poet live
Till ye come back; think what you do, you see   25
What audiences we have, what company
To Shakespeare comes, whose mirth did once beguile
Dull hours and, buskined, made even sorrow smile;
So lovely were the wounds that men would say
They could endure the bleeding a whole day;   30
He has but few friends lately, think o' that,
He'll come no more, and others have his fate.
Fletcher, the Muses' darling and choice love
Of Phoebus, the delight of every grove;
Upon whose head the laurel grew, whose wit   35
Was the time's wonder and example, yet
'Tis within memory, trees did not throng,
As once the story said, to Orpheus' song.
Jonson, t'whose name wise art did bow, and wit
Is only justified by honouring it;   40
To hear whose touch, how would the learned quire
With silence stoop! And when he took his lyre,
Apollo dropped his lute, ashamed to see
A rival to the god of harmony.
You do forsake him too; we must deplore   45
This fate, for we do know it by our door.
How must this author fear then, with his guilt
Of weakness, to thrive here, where late was spilt
The Muses' own blood, if being but a few,
You not conspire and meet more frequent too!   50
There are not now nine Muses, and you may
Be kind to ours; if not, he bade me say,
  Though while you careless kill the rest and laugh,
  Yet he may live to write your epitaph.

26. audiences] *Poems, etc.;* audience *Oct.*   27–30, 33–6, and 39–44] *In italics
and quotation marks, Poems, etc.*

27–30.] Armstrong believes the pointing to be gnomic.
27. *Shakespeare*] Cf. Hall's verses to Shirley, which do not mention
Shakespeare. The dramatists mentioned in ll. 27, 33 and 39 indicate
that the King's Men still relied on their 'glorious past' (Bentley, *Profession,* p. 223).
34. *Phoebus*] Apollo, god of music and poetry.
37–8. *trees ... song*] Orpheus's music is supposed to have moved
rocks and trees.
46. *our door*] the size of our audience.

This setting of 'Strephon and Daphne, a dialogue' was printed in John Playford's *The Musical Companion*, 2nd edition (London, 1673), pp. 63–4, and must surely be the original music for Shirley's song. The composer was William Lawes (1602–45), brother of Henry Lawes who collaborated with Milton in *Comus*. There are twenty-three songs and catches by Lawes in the 1673 edition of *The Musical Companion* (see Murray Lefkowitz, *William Lawes*, London, 1960). The verbal text here given differs in a few respects from that included in the play. Spelling has been modernised but punctuation and capitalisation are as in the original.

Glossarial Index to the Commentary

Words are generally cited in the form in which they appear in the text but where a word occurs in different forms the basic form only is given. An asterisk indicates information which supplements that found in O.E.D.

Abuse, V.iii.275
affects, I.ii.51
after, V.ii.21
agent, III.ii.190
allow, IV,ii.273
and, IV.ii.201
applied, III.ii.165
arras, II.iii.148
arrived, I.ii.72
art, I.i.32, V.iii.249
assassinate, III.ii.105
at his devotion, V.ii.66
at opportunity, V.ii.116

Babe, V.i.39
balk, IV.ii.202
basely, IV.ii.175
becoming, V.iii.292
be happy, I.ii.228
*behave, I.ii.158
behind, I.ii.11
believed, IV.ii.320
beshrew, V.iii.10
bill, *Prologue*,15
blood, I.i.29
bold, II.i.103
brave, III.ii.112
bravo, IV.iii.47
bride, I.i.7
burning glasses, II.iii.77

Cabled up, IV,ii.59
carkanet, IV.ii.84

carried, III.ii.48
cast, V.ii.131
castle, III.ii.245
censure, IV.ii.117
challenge, III.ii.151, IV.ii.282
chamber, V.iii.126
chaplets, V.iii.18, V.iii.105
character, I.ii.110, II.iii.37
charming, V.ii.94
chronicle, II.iii.43
circumstance, III.ii.170, V.i.94
clap, *Epilogue*,21
cleared, I.ii.12
*close, V.iii.75
clouds, III.ii.37
coarser blood, I.i.29
cock, V.iii.55
complexion, II.i.141
compose, I.i.43
*composition, I.ii.46. (cf. I.ii.37)
confederate, I.i.57
conference, I.ii.89
confines, I.i.54
confirmed, II.i.76
constable, III.ii.78
contracted, II.iii.127
conversation, *Dedication*,5
counted, III.i.42
cousin, IV.i.33
coxcomb, III.ii.21
creatures, V.ii.84
crutches, III.ii.174
cum privilegio, V.ii.38